Campus & Community

Moore Ruble Yudell   Architecture & Planning

Oscar Riera Ojeda

James Mary O'Connor

Wendy Kohn

Rockport Publishers

Rockport, Massachusetts

Campus & Community

Moore Ruble Yudell   Architecture & Planning

DEDICATION   This monograph is dedicated to Charles W. Moore, our teacher, partner, and friend. Charles' life and work are an inspiration to generations of architects and planners around the world, who share his humanistic concern for habitation and community, and his profound joy in creating places which celebrate the human spirit.

First published in the United States of America by:

Rockport Publishers, Inc.

146 Granite Street

Rockport, Massachusetts 01966-1299

Telephone: (508) 546-9590

Fax: (508) 546-7141

Distribution by:

Rockport Publishers, Inc.

Rockport, Massachusetts 01966-1299

ISBN 1-56496-230-X

10 9 8 7 6 5 4 3 2 1

Printed in Hong Kong by:

Regent Publishing Services Limited

To Jorge Iturrieta, Warren James, Alfredo Karan, Larry Lebeau, Michelle Saulnier, and Jorge Zuelgaray
O. R. O.

Graphic Design: Oscar Riera Ojeda

Composition: Matt Kanaracus/Codesign

Preface: "Building Ideals" by Wendy Kohn   6

Introduction: "Going to College" by Witold Rybczynski   8

Essay: "On Campus-Making in America" by Stefanos Polyzoides   11

WORKS

University of Oregon Science Complex   18
19   Reflections on the Project by Donlyn Lyndon
San Antonio Art Institute   32

Humboldt Bibliothek   40

Peter Boxenbaum Arts Education Centre, Crossroads School   52

UCSD Cellular and Molecular Medicine East & West   60
61   Reflections on the Project by Rob Quigley
Walter A. Haas School of Business Administration   76
77   Reflections on the Project by Diane Favro
California Center for the Arts, Escondido   90

University of Washington Chemistry Building   110
111   Reflections on the Project by Stephen Harby and Comments by Tallman Trask
Powell Library Renovation, UC Los Angeles   122
123   Reflections on the Project by Duke Oakley

ON CAMPUS AND COMMUNITY

"The Shape of Community" by Buzz Yudell   132

"Communities of Purpose" by John Ruble   136

"Real Accidents" Interview with John Ruble and Buzz Yudell   140

IN PROGRESS

Hugh and Hazel Darling Law Library Addition   146

Avery House, California Institute of Technology   156

Maryland Center for Performing Arts, University of Maryland   162
163   Reflections on the Project by Roger Lewis and Stephen Hurtt
Tacoma Campus Master Plan, University of Washington   176
177   Reflections on the Project by Stephen Harby and Comments by Tallman Trask
Shanghai Grand Theatre Design   184

Dong-Hwa National University Campus Master Plan   194

Kao-Shiung National Institute of Technology Campus Master Plan Design   202

APPENDIX

Project Credits   210

Chronology of Projects   212

Biographies, Awards, Exhibitions, & Publications   220

Note from the Architects   224

PREFACE

For many today, thinking about the architecture of community would begin with the conceptual structure of the World Wide Web. Our fastest-growing communities are immaterial, and the most vital discussions of architecture tend to regard the "architects" of new computer software or foreign policy agreements. Indeed, these new meanings for two old words are thrilling. Who would not want to "build" ideas with architectural elegance and tectonic structure? Who is not fascinated by what is effectively magic: the ability to take part in a virtual twenty-four-hour global community—unencumbered by our bodies and their organic requirements?

But while we continue to invent ever more sophisticated ways of countering nature's constraints, the cries for "lost community" in our cities and suburbs are getting louder. And as new buildings rarely achieve the power to symbolize and inspire today's society, architects debate whether there remains any role for their profession at all—publishing books with such titles as *Digital City, De-Architecture*, and not rhetorically, *The End of Architecture?*

Such responses to today's actual conditions are not only appropriate, but in fact, they are deeply reassuring. They remind us that the immediacy of human contact cannot be replaced by machines, however powerful. They attest that true community still requires real places to take root. And they suggest that if architects are listening, an urgent call for their services is to be heard.

Taking up the challenge to rejoin the concept of "community" with architectural shape and form requires that we use all the tools of analysis, design, and precedent available to us. In the United States, we find a unique resource for this work: the American college campus. Founded originally to exist aside from daily public life, American campuses constitute places in which that elusive quality of community has been protected and sustained. And yet, educational ideals aside, university campuses remain inescapably part of the "real" world. Subject to constrained budgets and conflicting interest groups; entrenched leaders and shifting populations; antagonistic neighbors and struggles to maintain identity—as well as the familiar stresses of present urgency challenging prudent planning—campuses share real-world constraints with towns and cities that we currently recognize as communities destroyed.

The pages that follow present the work of Moore Ruble Yudell, architects who have long believed in the power of architecture to foster human interaction. With international experience in balancing the exigencies of the "real" world with the opportunity to give shape to philosophical ideals, Moore Ruble Yudell has designed numerous campus buildings, cultural institutions, and new communities that remain equally sensitive to the people and buildings inside and outside the perimeter of their sites.

This volume focuses on the inhabitation of real places: at the urban and campus scale; at the site and building scale; at the scale of a single individual in the embrace of a community. Architects, writers, historians, campus planners, clients, and colleagues construct a context for this inquiry into the nature of campus communities today, and discuss as case studies planning and building projects on some of the oldest and most well-known campuses in the United States. Finally, in their essays and an interview, partners John Ruble and Buzz Yudell describe their own understanding of designing places deeply connected to society, which are rich in invention but respectful of history, and focused intensely upon the very subtle but very urgent goal of building vital, durable communities.

BUILDING IDEALS by Wendy Kohn

1	2	3
	5	6
4		9
7	8	

1 UCSD Cellular and Molecular Medicine West Wing 2 Walter A. Haas School of Business Administration 3 California Center for the Arts, Escondido
4 University of Oregon Science Complex 5 San Antonio Art Institute 6 The Peter Boxenbaum Arts Education Center
7 University of Washington Chemistry Building 8 Powell Library Renovation 9 Humboldt Bibliothek

I've never seen a "Sorbonne" sticker on a Citroën or a "London School of Economics" decal on a Rover, but in my Philadelphia, Pennsylvania neighborhood, station wagons are commonly adorned with names like "Dartmouth" and "Millersville U." As far as I know, this is the only country in the world where parents regularly display the name of their children's college or university on their car's rear window. This academic showing off has a lot to do with indirectly announcing status in a society purporting to be classless. But there's more to it than that. It's not only Ivy League names that are featured, after all, but also those of lesser-known schools like Millersville. Sometimes both appear on the same car, a cruelly public announcement of sibling rivalry. Yet "going to college" is not chiefly—or, at least, not only—about having been accepted by a prestigious institution. It's not merely about education. It's a rite of passage.

Going to college in America means going *away* to college. It means leaving home and family, usually for the first time. College socializes rebellious teenagers and teaches self-reliance. It introduces the student to a wider world, not only of people and ideas, but also of places. Thus it's an introduction to a predominant aspect of modern American life: mobility. The college is usually far from home, often in another state, and so students experience the immensity of the nation firsthand. They become commuters, traveling home for Thanksgiving or driving to Florida during spring break. For most of them, this perambulating habit will persist throughout their lives.

College is a sort of interlude between adolescence and adulthood, making it a world apart. Not surprisingly, this world's physical design reveals a great deal about society's values and views on life. Jefferson's "academical village" at the University of Virginia represents an Enlightenment attitude to education. Nineteenth-century New England colleges like Smith—with its serious architecture and picturesque Frederick Law Olmsted landscaping—combine a romantic view of youth with an admirable belief in the uplifting power of natural beauty. On the other hand, a Beaux-Arts campus like Henry Hornbostel's formal plan for Carnegie-Mellon University in Pittsburgh reflects a different ideal, one that was directly influenced by the 1893 Columbian Exposition. Here, the university became a Classical citadel of learning. Even utilitarian campuses of the 1950s "boom years," when colleges and universities expanded like wildfire, still resonate with a touching, crew-cut optimism about technology and the future, though they often resemble factories rather than academic enclaves.

The atmosphere has changed again today. Faith in the invincibility of learning is tarnished; many old institutional and curricular certainties have been called into question. Even the divisions between disciplines, those disciplines upon which the university's organization is founded, are eroding just like the line between theory and practice in academic pursuits. The outside world has intruded. Politics, morality, and social debate have become a part of academic life, sometimes with a vengeance. On the whole, the university has embraced these changes and, in the process, abandoned the ivory tower.

The architects of contemporary campus buildings are faced with a challenging problem: embodying this new outlook in their designs and making campuses into places that address the diversity and uncertainty of learning today. It would be easy enough to design campuses comprising merely serviceable, flexible office buildings, the sort of environment that Candilis, Josic, and Woods created for the Free University of Berlin. Built in 1963, this anonymous and interchangeable structure resembles a large airport terminal. But that would hardly do for an American campus. Such bureaucratic rationality lacks the requisite sense of place and particular identity that going to college still demands. Recreating a campus setting of the past—as neo-Gothic architects did in the early 1900s at Yale, Princeton, and West Point—would undoubtedly offer a more attractive environment, but it would not provide the appropriate imagery for the uncloistered university of today. Something else is needed.

Charles Moore successfully identified that "something else" as early as 1965 when he designed Kresge College (in association with Donlyn Lyndon, William Turnbull, and Richard Whitaker) for the University of California at Santa Cruz. Kresge College introduced an important idea to university planning: the campus building as a kind of town. This is not to be confused with Jefferson's formal academical village, nor with Eero Saarinen's Morse and Stiles colleges at Yale, which were completed in 1962 and together resemble a rough-hewn Mediterranean village. To Moore and his associates, "town" meant something different. The dorms, which programmatically might have been accommodated in a single structure, were housed in more than a dozen buildings, artfully arranged across the sloping site. The focus was not a quadrangle or a park, however, but a thousand-foot-long winding street. The result is reminiscent of an American Main Street. The buildings at Kresge reflect another aspect of the small town: the highway strip. The architectural details recall motels: there are bits of neon lighting, bright colors, and street lamps. The chief social space is not a chapel or a library, but a laundromat. It is all playful rather than serious, and it produces a jumbled, unstructured, and informal setting that makes the educational institution less, well, institutional.

Moore established the Los Angeles-based office of Moore Ruble Yudell with John Ruble and Buzz Yudell in 1979.

Their campus work, which is extremely varied in scale and program, has a common thread: it elaborates and expands on Moore's original intuition. All these projects are broken down into parts (as in Kresge, parts that are not necessarily determined by function), and are then arranged to create what can only be called townplaces. In a sense, they belong as much to urbanism as to architecture.

The Walter A. Haas School of Business at the University of California, Berkeley has none of Kresge's honky-tonk features; it is, after all, a business school. It is also, however, a collection of linked buildings defining an irregular outdoor space. At the San Antonio Art Institute, an art college in Texas, the expression, once more, is of a collection of buildings rather than a single form. Here, the architects create a public square *inside* the building. The Molecular Biology Research Facility at the University of California, San Diego consists of two functionally constrained blocks, but the designers manage to make the focus a miniature square by pulling out the conference room in a freestanding tower and interposing an exterior staircase and giant pergola. The result is a quite beautiful group that combines practicality with whimsy.

Moore Ruble Yudell's first large, significantly complicated project was the Science Complex of the University of Oregon in Eugene. What might have been a single block is designed as five free-standing structures integrated with existing buildings. The whole complex is traversed by a pedestrian walk punctuated by staircases, fountains, arcades, bridges, and small plazas. The heart of the project is an urban space of a different sort, one familiar to users of hotels and office complexes: the atrium.

The theme of a multi-centered complex is explored further in the recent competition-winning design for a performing arts center for the University of Maryland at College Park, the first major project begun by the firm after Charles Moore's untimely demise. The 300,000-square-foot building includes five separate performance spaces and manages the difficult task, in the words of the competition jury, of being a monumentally scaled landmark for the public and a humanely scaled facility for students and faculty. The lobby of the Center for the Performing Arts is a contemporary place, both casual in organization and spatially exciting. Yet, the urbanism espoused by Moore Ruble Yudell is resolutely traditional; that is, buildings are never conceived as sculptural objects in space (in the modernist manner) but, rather, as plastic objects that define and enclose space.

This is particularly evident at an urban scale in two ambitious master plans: a new branch campus in Tacoma for the University of Washington and Dong-Hwa University in Hwa-Lien, Taiwan. In the Tacoma project, the master plan carefully reinforces the existing street pattern by controlling the location and height of new buildings. At Dong-Hwa, a brand new university campus for 10,000 students, courtyard buildings situated in a regular grid of streets and boulevards are broken by a meandering series of connected ponds and lakes. When it is complete, this promises to be a memorable, town-like campus.

In the past, American campus architecture could be clearly identified by its style: James Gamble Rogers's Gothic at Yale, Charles A. Coolidge's Romanesque at Stanford, or Charles Follen McKim's Beaux-Arts Classicism at Columbia. Charles Moore is generally known as one of the originators of Post-Modernism, and there are reminders of that style in the work of Moore Ruble Yudell, especially in their pragmatic approach to history and in their eclectics' delight in combining and recombining architectural motifs. And yet it seems to me that it would be a mistake to label these architects Post-Modernists. Buildings like the University of Washington Chemistry Building, the Cal Tech Science & Engineering Library, or Avery House, also at Cal Tech, are architecturally straight-faced, both in massing and detail. On the other hand, the University of Oregon Science Complex and one of their most accomplished designs, the Walter A. Haas School of Business, take apart and reassemble architectural elements in a way that could be called Deconstructionist, if that label were not already used to describe a very different— and considerably less humanistic and engaging—approach to architectural design.

In regard to the work of Moore Ruble Yudell it is perhaps more accurate to speak of architectural *character* than of architectural style. Theirs is a rich palette of materials, forms, and colors. The firm is not afraid to use explicit historical references and decorative motifs. Robert A.M. Stern once criticized the architecture of Kresge College for being too abstract, and for incorporating a sense of impermanence that mocked rather than glorified its student users. Irony was one of the least attractive characteristics of Post-Modernism, and it is absent in the work of Moore Ruble Yudell. Indeed, their most successful designs have little literary or metaphorical content. Unlike some contemporary architects who use architecture to make social or artistic statements, Moore Ruble Yudell is more interested in creating buildings that reinforce a sense of place.

If these buildings sometimes appear fragmentary (one of their chief charms), as if they were assembled out of bits and pieces, it may be because they are the result of what Buzz Yudell has called a "circle of collaboration." That circle has included more than the three architects, their associates, and staff. Moore Ruble Yudell has achieved something quite extraordinary in architecture: they have managed to combine design excellence with that old '60s ideal: user participation.

I don't mean simply asking clients what they want—all architects do that—but, through public workshops, involving users of buildings (in the case of campus buildings, that includes staff, faculty, and students) in the actual design process. "We like to listen," says Yudell. "We like to hear each other and we like to be criticized. We also extend that desire to listen and collaborate to our clients. We don't feel the need to have complete ownership, but we all feel ownership as a kind of collective, joint ownership." This is truly architecture as a social art, not merely because it provides a setting for society, but because it treats design itself as a collective, rather than personal, activity.

It is obviously no accident that Moore Ruble Yudell's architectural renderings, unlike those of many contemporary architects, almost always include human figures. These campus buildings are places in which the students look comfortable and unquestionably at home. There is more to this than meets the eye, although it strikes the eye first. This is not warmed-over corporate architecture, which can turn young men and women in T-shirts, shorts, and sneakers into raggedy interlopers. Nor is this an attempt to make the ivory tower into a kind of shopping mall: non-threatening but distinctly low-brow. This architecture manages to be both casual and substantial; relaxed and serious; ordered, but not coercive. This is not easy to do, and in my mind represents Moore Ruble Yudell's chief accomplishment.

Witold Rybczynski is the Martin and Margy Meyerson Professor of Urbanism at the University of Pennsylvania. He writes regularly for The Atlantic, The New York Review of Books, and The New York Times. He is the author of The Most Beautiful House in the World and Looking Around: A Journey Through Architecture. His new book is City Life: Urban Expectations in a New World.

ESSAY

In Chapter 3 of their seminal 1922 book *Civic Art,* Werner Hegemann and Elbert Peets described American campus urbanism with the title "The Grouping of Buildings in America." In telling contrast, in Chapter 2 they identified most of the great classical continental precedents for campuses as "Plaza and Court Design in Europe." It was their assertion that European urbanism was based on an aesthetic principle of arranging public space formally and figurally. American urbanism "differed entirely, having evolved over time..." through the informal, incremental production of individual buildings, and through them, the definition of fluid and ambiguous public space. Their observation that campus-making is a unique American cultural contribution and tradition is of profound and lasting value. This essay will probe the importance of that position to several current architectural and urbanist challenges.

What is constant in the building of the American university campus is the process of continuous physical change. American campus planning practice was born of a revolutionary, Jeffersonian view of humanity: a liberal education was viewed as a means for young Americans to defend their democratic freedoms over their lifetimes. In support of that goal, the campus was designed as an idealized setting: a city in the countryside or the countryside in a city. There, students were to be exposed to the civilizing powers of architecture to impart lessons of civic duty and community service. A campus education was intended to convince students of the necessity for tradition and the possibility of cultural evolution.

University of Virginia, Charlottesville, Thomas Jefferson, 1822; Courtesy University of Virginia Library.

United States Naval Academy, Annapolis, Maryland; Ernest Flagg. Courtesy University of Minnesota Archives.

United States Marine Corps Base, San Diego, California; Bertram Grosvenor Goodhue, 1917.

The architectural principles of campus urbanism in America are deeply embedded in the foundation of every university in the country begun before 1945. Many of these principles can be traced to the very beginnings of campus-making by Thomas Jefferson at the University of Virginia. Others have evolved in various forms since then. Architecture and urbanism imbued with these values express the best in the American character: valuing the familiar while exploring the new.

Despite the catastrophic disruption that the last two generations of building have wrought on every campus in the country, we now stand at an architectural crossroads. Clearance, sprawl, and the random juxtaposition of buildings that are the common campus pattern of today need to be replaced by an ethic of conservation and an aesthetic of judicious

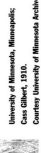

University of Minnesota, Minneapolis; Cass Gilbert, 1910. Courtesy University of Minnesota Archives.

11

infill design. The best traditions of American campus architecture and urbanism must be rediscovered as a prime source for generating architectural and campus form.

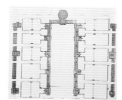

University of Virginia;
Thomas Jefferson, 1822.
Photo courtesy of Bill Sublette.
Plan courtesy of University of Virginia Library.

1. INTERCONNECTED, FLUID FIGURES OF OPEN SPACE

The word "campus" came into wide use as a 19th-century transformation of the Italian word *campo*. In the first universities of this country, the central group of buildings typically formed this emblematic space. The word described a shaped, public, open area—piazza—which was meant to be the central place and representation of the university. Eventually, as universities became larger and more complex, the term "campus" came to represent an aggregate and interconnected set of voids, the total figure of space in between the university's buildings. The word has now come to describe all of a university's grounds and buildings, the total physical presence of an institution.

The Arts Quad, Cornell University, Ithaca, New York.

University of Richmond, Virginia; Cram, Goodhue & Ferguson. Photo used with permission of Hoyle, Doran & Berry Inc., Boston.

The incremental formation of a figure of public space is essential to the scale and character of a campus. People who live and work in academic settings depend on the definition of a network of campus places to enrich both their daily lives and their senses of identity. Since the campus is constructed sequentially through individual projects that precisely define new elements of building, open space, and landscape, the whole is affected every time the smallest physical change takes place.

Princeton University, New Jersey; development plan by Ralph Adams Cram, 1906–1911. Courtesy of Architectural Drawings Collection, Princeton University Archives, Department of Rare Books and Special Collections, Princeton University Libraries.

A campus depends on a limited number of spatial types for its successful physical definition. Its design depends on the local climate and the particular culture of the place. These components range in size and architectural character from the small to the large, and from the simple to the complex:

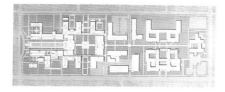

California Institute of Technology, Pasadena; recreated plan by Polyzoides and de Bretteville, 1988.

A patio is a room-sized space, no more than twenty feet on one side, and is typically an outdoor extension of a single room;

Cranbrook School for Boys, Bloomfield Hills, Michigan; Eliel Saarinen, 1925. Courtesy of Collection of Cranbrook Art Museum.

A courtyard is a space not more than one hundred feet on one side, is enclosed within a building, and is intended for exclusive use by a variety of rooms;

Scripps College. Claremont, California; recreated plan by Polyzoides and de Bretteville, 1988.

A quadrangle is a space not more than four hundred feet on one side, is distinct and finite, and is shared among many buildings;

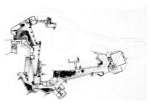

Reed College. Portland, Oregon; Doyle, Patterson & Beach, 1912. Courtesy of Reed College Archives.

A lawn or green is a space measured at the scale of the whole campus and which defines its ritual and symbolic center;

A field is a clearing dimensioned to accommodate athletic activities and is typically located on the edge of a campus.

2. A FABRIC OF CONTINUOUS BUILDING

By their location and form, buildings can define an interconnected, fluid figure of open space. They are permanent and essential physical presences. The stability of their exterior forms is a great deal more important than their floorplans. Further, their combined form as an ensemble is more important than the particular formal qualities of any one of them in isolation.

Through their useful lives, often counted in decades, campus buildings will be used for a variety of purposes. Continuity in massing, similarity in inflection, repetition of architectural elements and materials, and likeness in construction result in buildings fit to respond to the shifting circumstances of their use over time.

Fine Arts Building, Mills College; Walter H. Ratcliff, 1926.

Kresge College, University of California, Santa Cruz; Moore, Turnbull, Lyndon and Whitaker, 1974.

There are five types of buildings in a campus. The overall organization and image of a campus depends on the relationships between its buildings at any moment in time. Through unique design, each type generates a building of particular formal character:

Monumental buildings are unique in their symbolic importance. They do not represent any one academic discipline, and they tend to accommodate shared programs important to the entire academic community. Such buildings are prominently located. They tend to be the most physically and spatially idiosyncratic buildings on campus. Their plans and sections are complex and their elevations define them as individual objects. Their forms are emblematic of the history and the civic importance of the whole university;

Rice University: Administration Building, Houston, Texas; Cram, Goodhue and Ferguson, 1910.

Academic loft buildings are the most common and versatile of all campus buildings. They are regular in plan and section, and complex in elevation, as their exterior surfaces define the scale of the campus open spaces that they front. Most teaching and research activities take place in such buildings. They house a variety of departments representing different academic disciplines. They are adaptable over time and can be expanded with ease. They are the most ordinary building block of the campus and are found in all of its precincts;

Cranbrook School for Boys; Eliel Saarinen, 1925.

Laboratory loft buildings are a version of the academic loft, designed for unusually heavy requirements of mechanical supply and exhaust services. They are exclusively dedicated to housing the experimental sciences. Their internal spatial arrangements are fixed. Their exterior surfaces bear the most typical campus building responsibility: through gestures of inflection with neighboring buildings, they help form the various figures of open space that define the campus;

Physics Building, Rice University, Houston, Texas; Cram, Goodhue and Ferguson, 1915.

Residence halls are buildings that provide facilities for student living in what amounts to campus neighborhoods. Such buildings are organized like houses: each possesses a set of common public rooms for living, dining, reading, and recreation, surrounded by dozens of bedrooms organized in clusters around common bathrooms;

Swarthmore College: Women's Residential Complex, Pennsylvania; Karcher and Smith, 1922. Reprinted from Architectural Forum, June 1931, p.674.

Ancillary buildings comprise all other buildings dedicated to the infrastructure and transportation needs of a campus. Typically, such buildings are office lots, warehouse lots, or parking structures. They are of a routine form, located and designed in a manner that befits their temporary and utilitarian character.

Princeton University parking structure by Machado and Silvetti, 1988–1991.

3. A CULTIVATED LANDSCAPE

An understanding of the landscape as a language equal and parallel to the language of architecture has been a central aspect of the American campus-making tradition. The cultivated landscape in a campus is formally connected to all open spaces, not to its adjacent buildings. Its purpose is to define distinct settings for social interaction. By its size, form, color, texture, scale, and other architectural characteristics, it can strengthen the unity of the entire campus. The intimacy of patios, the engaging social character of courtyards, the formality of quads, the monumentality of greens, and the informality of fields are all defined through the architectural disposition of their landscape components.

Wellesley College, Massachusetts. Cram and Ferguson, 1916. Courtesy of Wellesley College Archives.

The found, natural qualities of a campus should be exploited to maximize its unique character. The physiognomy of the ground, the presence of the horizon and the sky, the native vegetation, and varying qualities of light are some of the most memorable ingredients for regionally specific place-making on the American continent.

A campus is a district of limited size, where ecological initiatives can be coupled with the aestheticization of nature. Recycling water, garbage, and sewage, using non-toxic materials and passive energy sources, conserving energy, and reusing buildings are all essential strategies for guaranteeing the health of the natural world of the campus.

Lewis & Clark College, Portland, Oregon; Herman Brookman, 1924.

Formally, the ground, walls, columns, canopies, individual rooms, and collective figures of "outdoor rooms" should be conceptualized through natural materials.

4. A COMPACT INFRASTRUCTURE

The American campus was developed originally as a compact, distinct academic district with a central focus, a defined perimeter, and a clear relationship to the town that surrounded it. As campuses grew, new projects were spaced further and further from campus centers, with separate precincts organized by location, use, and physical prominence. As cars became dominant, the scale of vehicular circulation and parking began to overwhelm the campus pedestrian. A development pattern that favored the design and construction of uncoordinated projects took hold. A form of campus evolved that was characterized by haphazard massing and horizontal over-extension, and which mimicked suburban sprawl.

University of Southern California, Los Angeles.

This expansion of campuses beyond their original boundaries required more land, roads, and utility extensions. It brought universities into conflict with the neighborhoods surrounding them. Campus walking distances increased as students living and studying at the edges were isolated from the shared activities at the heart of the campus. The spaces between buildings were enlarged and remained uninhabited. The figural open space of campuses increasingly eroded.

Campus sprawl can only be checked through the incremental development of open space, building, and landscape projects within pedestrian precincts. There are two means by which such places can be formed and maintained: first, by designing projects that are compact and close to existing development and which avoid excessive extension of infrastructure; second,

Rice University. Cram, Goodhue and Ferguson, 1910. University Archives, Woodson Research Center, Rice University Library.

by adopting the "parking-once principle." Campus users should be able to leave their cars and proceed through the activities of an entire day without needing to drive again.

A campus must remain a place where parking supports pedestrian access to precincts, not to individual buildings. These precincts then remain connected by pedestrian circulation through well-defined and beautiful realms of public space.

5. TYPOLOGICAL UNITY AND STYLISTIC VARIETY

The conceptual strategies for forming a coherent American campus rest on the recognition of the campus as a built pedestrian district. Individual projects should contribute to the creation of one of the following three kinds of campus order: Infill—adjusting buildings and places within existing campus precinct boundaries; Completion—designing projects that complete the form of existing campus precincts; Extension—expanding the campus by defining both the form of new precincts and the rules for achieving precinct completion over time.

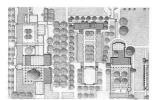

Scripps College. Recreated plan by Moule and Polyzoides.

Under current architectural practice, there are several dominant ways of generating campus form. Based on the specific parameters of their program and site, individual projects are often prescribed within a narrow stylistic range. The result is a sense of false continuity, verging on the banal. At the opposite end of the spectrum, architects are allowed to introduce projects expressed in deeply personal styles, most often of an exaggerated, monumental presence. In both cases, obsession with style—on the one hand narrowly dictating it, on the other encouraging it without limit—precludes any possibility of producing a campus as a collective form of buildings, open space, and landscape. The result is a state of visual disorder and psychic confusion.

Highland District, University of Arizona in Tucson; Moule and Polyzoides, 1990.

A typological approach to campus-making represents the ultimate balance between architectural and urbanist ideals: to build a unified campus of diverse parts. Typological continuity allows projects to share architectural elements and to function cohesively in creating a public realm. Formal compatibility then sets up a campus that remains not only visually coherent, but conceptually articulate in its development over time.

Architectural diversity is truly meaningful only when read against a backdrop of formal continuity that transcends any one individual project. Indeed, a coherent architectural context is a condition for unique expression. Therefore, the discipline inherent in a campus structure that is defined typologically *supports* stylistic variety.

6. INCOMPLETE BUILDINGS AND COMPLETE DISTRICTS

In the era of the master plan, buildings became the dominant component of campus-making. Open space was devalued and landscape was most often used as an afterthought to minimize the damage so often inflicted by buildings.

Morse and Stiles Colleges, Yale University, New Haven, Connecticut; Eero Saarinen, 1960.

With buildings most often conceived as pieces of a fixed puzzle, the ultimate form of the puzzle was to be achieved by the contributions of a variety of designers. Buildings were designed in fashionable isolation; their architects covered an ever-widening aesthetic spectrum, and inflexible master plans failed to keep pace with campus development.

These developments in our time have been disastrous. Assemblies of isolated and formally hermetic buildings have produced blatantly incomplete campus precincts and frayed entire campuses.

The alternative to the current state of campus dissonance is a radical reversal of architectural priorities. The fixed master plan should be replaced by a physical framework that differentiates between the urban form of the campus as a whole and the opportunity for incremental, circumstantial design shifts within it. Regulating plans and sections should define road, parking, utility, open space, and landscape configurations as the permanent physical order of a campus. On a compulsory basis, individual projects should contribute to the design of these campus elements.

By contrast, the design of a particular building should be regulated by a simple code that establishes its typological character through the essential issues of form, density, and use.

The purpose of architectural design for campuses must transcend the design of individual buildings. Buildings and projects must be designed in a less self-sufficient, less resolute form. Over time, adjacent buildings can share architectural elements through repetition, inflection, or contrast. The formal incompleteness of projects can then become the source of ever more complete precincts, and harmonious, evolving, collective campus form.

After the urbanist responsibilities and the deep character of individual buildings have been established, their design can remain a matter of aesthetic judgment by individual architects.

7. AN INTEGRATED PROCESS OF DEVELOPMENT

Great projects and great campuses are contingent upon the definition of a thoroughly integrated, multi-party process of development. The academic leadership of universities should encourage the traditional notion of a campus as a teaching instrument and as an expression of the community whose purpose is aimed toward the society as a whole. It should rally academic representatives to the planning and design process to make decisions that benefit that collective purpose, not one particular fief. It should lead a process of realistic budgeting that leads to permanent facilities in the form of 50- to 75-year buildings. It should be directly involved in the judicious choice of architects based on established competence, perhaps determined by limited competition. It should ensure that the process of campus planning and building is collaborative, not adversarial.

Campus planning and campus facility construction bureaucracies need to be streamlined. They must operate under the same constraints of time and responsibility as their architects. Their mandate must be changed from a defense of the bottom line to the pursuit of designing a campus worthy of its name, with buildings that meet the test of time, both physically and culturally. Who remembers the meaningless management battles surrounding the construction of buildings even a day after their completion?

The complex subject of campus-making in America cannot be entrusted to architects alone. At the same time, architects should be offered the substantial respect, support, and collaboration of the institutions that they serve. Campus-making should be *led* by architects, and involve the active collaboration of a variety of design and engineering professionals. The separation of architectural commissions into design and construction phases to be carried out by different firms constitutes an ongoing attack on architects by irreparably splitting their responsibilities. This development undermines the long-term viability of the entire architectural profession. Further, the division of commissions into parts such as programming and construction management, carried out by para-architects, separates the final design of buildings from decisions that can and should be crucial to their proper formation. Architecture is inherently an integrated discipline; architects need to remain the masters of a whole built product, based on a complete range of knowledge and responsibility.

IN PURSUIT OF COHERENCE
We live in the midst of a deeply divided architectural culture. Its two poles claim opposing ideals and directions. At one pole, the proponents of a perpetual cultural revolution claim that the goal of architecture should be the invention of ever-fresh, unique, and monumental architectural form; at the other, the proponents of historicist continuity claim that the cultural rifts of this century can only be healed by the discovery and repetition of expressions past.

In the middle, and within a very narrow band, a few architects claim a ground that preserves the prerogatives of both newness and continuity. Understanding for the deep architectural traditions of the country, respect for the human purposes of architecture, and deep sensitivity to place and to nature are the sources of our most inspired practice.

The notion of coherence is central to understanding this third way of framing architecture and urbanism. Awareness of history and culture leads to transformation of precedent. Order resides not only in the poetry endowed in the design of individual things, but in their connections to cultures and places, and in their ability to become points of departure for new form. Newness can be synonymous with subtlety and with cultural shifts that enrich instead of alienate.

The American campus-making tradition is an invaluable source of coherence, the source of many wondrous future projects, and a guarantee for the survival of the American university as an institution of coherence and meaning.

Few American firms have recognized this fundamental professional truth. One that has produced buildings deeply and consistently based on this principle is Moore Ruble Yudell. Its work is rooted in the efforts of Charles Moore over his lifetime to remember historical places and to clarify architectural precedents as an inspiration for current practice. His constant promoting of an American architecture based on an inventive reinterpretation of regional cultural traditions has profoundly affected Moore Ruble Yudell's work.

For John Ruble and Buzz Yudell, the discovery of the American campus as a source of rich formal architectural and urbanist lessons is part of a larger pattern. It is a natural outcome of their distinctive aesthetic and ethical professional posture: to seek coherence in all its formal manifestations. Their mastery over the subject matter of architecture endows their work with that sign of poetry's presence: architectural form whose character moves the spirit. Of course, there is nothing about the Moore Ruble Yudell campus building projects illustrated here that is simplistic in form or random in process. The architectural realism of the firm's approach is based on a practice that professes a very particular way of designing and being, which includes:

Knowledge—The projects are informed by an awareness of history, and by travel around the world as firsthand experience of buildings and places. Moore Ruble Yudell is a literate and intellectual office where reading, writing, and speaking are a central aspect of the act of analyzing intentions, evaluating precedents, and designing buildings;

Thought—The projects are finely balanced between a sense of the whole and the design of their parts. Their conceptual value lies in the designers' insistence that architecture is still an integrative expression. Program and site, space and structure, surface and light, building and garden, and material and energy are juxtaposed in a struggle to force new experience and new meaning through building form;

Feeling—The projects are endowed with a profound lyricism. The particular design of both their space and material form is figural in a manner that engages the human body, thoughts, and emotions in an empathetic relationship. This is an architecture of sensual pleasure and spiritual connectedness. It is designed to be uplifting and worthy of the affection of the people using it;

Service—The projects are deeply related to the needs and wishes of the individuals and the institutions that sponsor

them. They are often designed with the active participation of client groups. In all cases, they are built with the conviction that the act of dwelling is the ultimate confirmation of the validity of architectural form. To experience a Moore Ruble Yudell building is to experience a rich feeling of modesty and of humanity.

This volume is a salute to the ability of Charles Moore, John Ruble, Buzz Yudell, and their talented staff to draw the idealistic, the unconventional, and the unexpected from the conditions of each of their projects. The poetry of their finished work speaks eloquently to the ability of architecture to remain a powerful guide to the human spirit as it continues to chart a course between the familiar and the unknown.

Stephanos Polyzoides leads a practice in architecture and urbanism with Elizabeth Moule. They are authors of several books and articles on architecture and urban design and are both founders of the Congress for the New Urbanism. He currently teaches architecture at the University of Southern California.

BIBLIOGRAPHY

Christ-Janer, Albert, *Eliel Saarinen,* The University of Chicago Press, Chicago and London, 1948.

Fox, Stephen, "The General Plan of the William M. Rice Institute and Its Architectural Development," in *Architecture at Rice, Monograph 29,* School of Architecture, Rice University, Houston, 1980.

Hays, Michael, *Unprecedented Realism: The Architecture of Machado and Silvetti,* Princeton Architectural Press, New York, 1995.

Hegemann, Werner, and Elbert Peets, *Civic Art,* Princeton Architectural Press, New York, 1922, 1988.

Klauder, Charles Z., and Herbert C. Wise, *College Architecture in America,* Charles Scribner's Sons, New York, 1929.

Larson, Jens Fredrick, and Archie MacInnes Palmer, *Architectural Planning of the American College,* McGraw-Hill Book Co., Inc., New York and London, 1933.

Turner, Paul Venable, *Campus: An American Planning Tradition,* The MIT Press, Cambridge, Mass., 1984.

Whitaker, Charles Harris, *Bertram Grosvenor Goodhue: Architect and Master of Many Arts,* Press of the American Institute of Architects, Inc., New York, 1925. Da Capo Press, New York, 1976.

White, Theo B., *Paul Philippe Cret,* The Art Alliance Press, Philadelphia, 1970.

Wilson, Richard Guy, ed., *Thomas Jefferson's Academical Village,* Bayly Art Museum, University Press of Virginia, Charlottesville, 1993.

The Work of Cram and Ferguson, Architects, The Pencil Points Press, Inc., New York, 1929.

The University of Oregon Science Complex functions in multiple ways. The four buildings composing the complex are discrete, free-standing buildings that house individual departments, organized vertically. They also connect horizontally to help form the interdisciplinary relationships that are critical to the way the sciences function. Bridges between departments house the offices of interdisciplinary institutes. More informal connection is made along a science walk that links all buildings through arches and courts.

Each building has a series of important social spaces, from informal areas near clustered offices to departmental hearths and courtyards. The heart of the project is a four-story atrium, bounded by classrooms, conference spaces, research laboratories, and institutes. This and other major meeting areas are designed to maximize a south-facing orientation, especially important in the climate of the American Northwest.

Laboratories, offices, and social spaces all evolved in close response to the nature of research and communication. The scientists collaborated with Moore Ruble Yudell in workshops

UNIVERSITY OF OREGON SCIENCE COMPLEX

Eugene, Oregon

to model their specific research patterns and needs. A flat-slab concrete structural system maximizes flexibility in planning the laboratory bays, and overhead mechanical services allow for easy lab set-up.

New science buildings infill the site to create positively defined entries and courtyards along the main campus spine. "Science Walk" provides a secondary path for faculty and students.

The University of Oregon campus was initiated in the second half of the 19th century by a proud vertical structure decked out in Francophile garb, and processed through the eastern United States. This was the College. A distant cousin of the Old Boston City Hall and distantly related to the Old Executive Office Building next to the White House, this original building resembles a dozen or more other American structures that were the first buildings of most land-grant institutions. Only later did the campus expand into multiple structures perched around an open green.

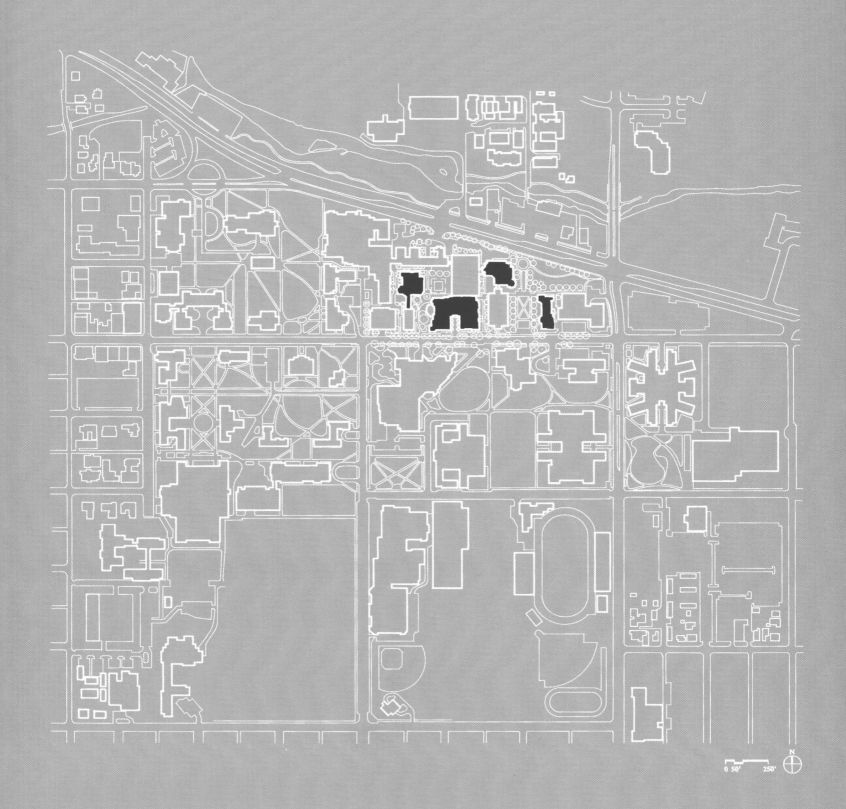

0 50'   250'   N

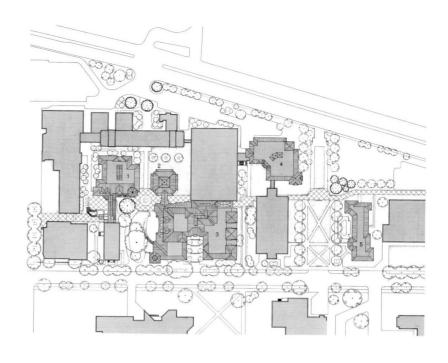

1. Cascade Hall (geology)
2. Science Library (proposed)
3. Willamette Hall (physics)
4. Streisinger Hall (biology)
5. Deschutes Hall (computer science)

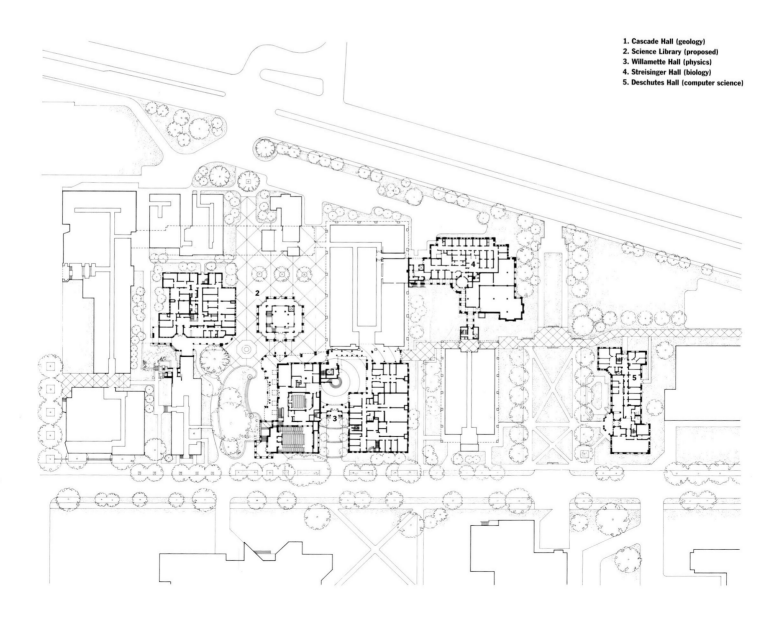

The second phase of building, under the guidance of Ellis Lawrence, was definitive to the campus as we now know it. Lawrence conceived buildings that shaped the spaces beyond them. He created the image of the campus as a coordinated, unified group of buildings, which individually might take different shapes, but together share a common vision. His was a campus of grand spaces, dignified brick buildings, and craftsmanship. The library, museum, and gymnasium he built all stand up to the best in American campus design—and do so with both invention and becoming modesty.

The post-World War II architecture was not so kind to the Oregon campus, intent as it was on flouting tradition and expressing modernity with concrete, steel, and glass, and little knowledge of weathering (and in the case of one major science building, a structure that bounced!). These buildings sat uncomfortably on their sites and did little to help the campus around them, even when they tried. Later, more sophisticated designs were more sympathetic to the earlier brick tradition, but remained, like the student center, isolated buildings alone on their sites.

Christopher Alexander's Oregon Experiment work, adopted as the basis for a campus-wide planning process under the guidance of Dean Robert Harris, changed the thrust of planning, setting campus "repair" as a priority. This process, with the active involvement of faculty and staff in all stages of planning, set the stage for Moore Ruble Yudell and the Ratcliff Architects to launch a truly brilliant renaissance of the campus building tradition. At ease with the collaborative exchange anticipated by the Oregon Experiment, the architects were able to make a place rich with nuance and imagination, capturing opportunities to nurture the complex interactions that the university's science community specifically sought.

The buildings that have resulted are at once subdued and exhilarating. The design creates a series of well-formed indoor and outdoor spaces that extends the reach of the civilized campus into areas once discarded or reserved for parking lots. Along the way, the architects have assimilated several of the most intransigent object buildings, setting existing buildings on the site into purposeful contexts. The general massing of the complex sits so comfortably along the street that it seems hard to imagine it otherwise; it's almost matter-of-fact.

But then there are the inevitable sparklers, the jots of pleasure sprinkled through the site, the lodging places for memory. These result from unexpected shapings of form, as in the entry pavilion to the lecture hall or the great carved porch facing the largest courtyard; from spaces like the central atrium that joins several buildings under one roof, or the open stairs climbing through upper levels of the geology and biology buildings. More pointedly, a series of collaborations with artists have made distinctive places at several locations throughout the site. Kent Bloomer's flickering molecular structures in the ceiling of the Atrium, Scott Wylie's intricately laid paving stones along Science Walk, and Wayne Chabre's bronze busts throughout the building make places and image distinct, providing for rich associations.

These structures hold up the prospect that, in diversity and accommodation, Moore Ruble Yudell has found the path to architecture that really matters—important to its inhabitants and in consort with its surroundings. Sparked by particularities of vision and fused by a consistency in building method and proportion, the project invites us to live fully in this place. The buildings of the University of Oregon Science Complex gain their authority from the imagination invested in them and from the intensity of care they reveal, not from the trappings of a given garb, be it Modern, Post-Modern, Classical, or Francophile.

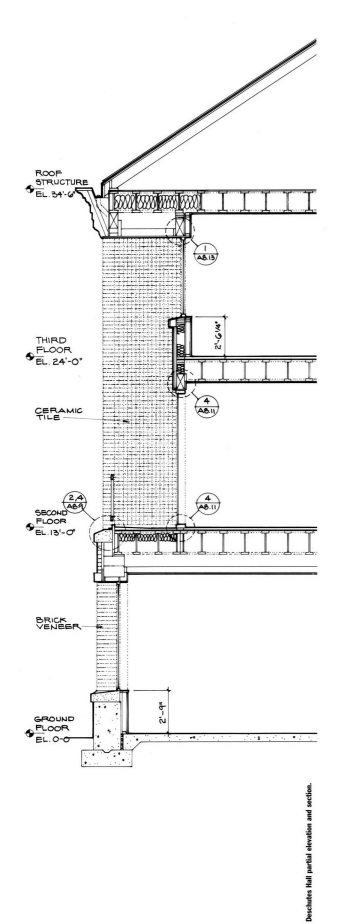

ROOF
STRUCTURE
EL. 34'-6"

1
A8.13

THIRD
FLOOR
EL. 24'-0"

2'-6 1/4"

4
A8.11

CERAMIC
TILE

2,4
A8.9

4
A8.11

SECOND
FLOOR
EL. 13'-0"

BRICK
VENEER

2'-9"

GROUND
FLOOR
EL. 0-0

Deschutes Hall partial elevation and section.

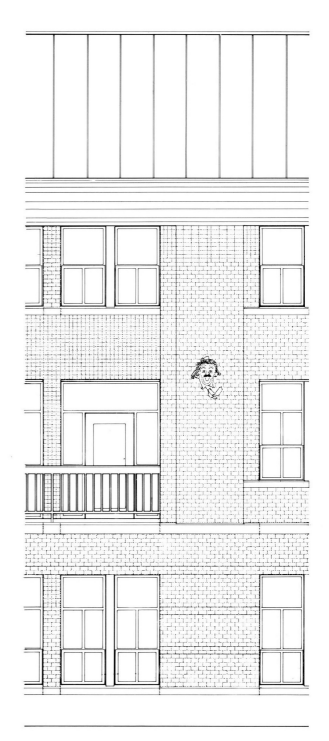

Geology Court; fountain designed by Alice Wingwall.

Porch column details, Willamette Hall.

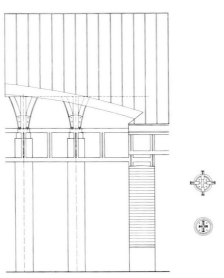

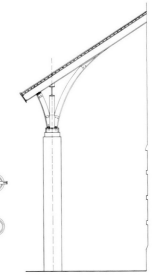

Elevator and stair details, Willamette Hall atrium.

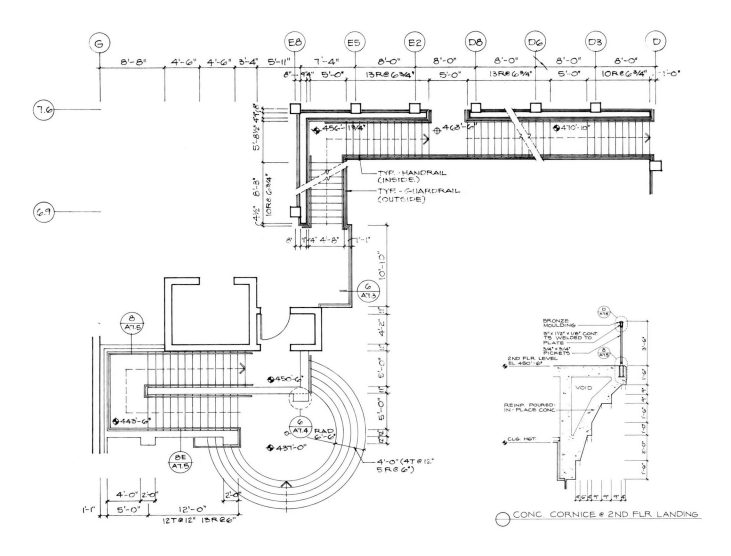

TYP. HANDRAIL
(INSIDE.)

TYP. GUARDRAIL
(OUTSIDE)

BRONZE
MOULDING

3" x 1½" x ⅛" CONT.
TS WELDED TO
PLATE

¾" x ¾"
PICKETS

2ND FLR LEVEL
EL. 450'-6"

VOID

REINF. POURED-
IN-PLACE CONC.

CLG. HGT.

CONC. CORNICE @ 2ND FLR LANDING

RAD
6'-6"

4'-0" (4T @ 12"
5 R @ 6")

12 T @ 12"   13 R @ 6"

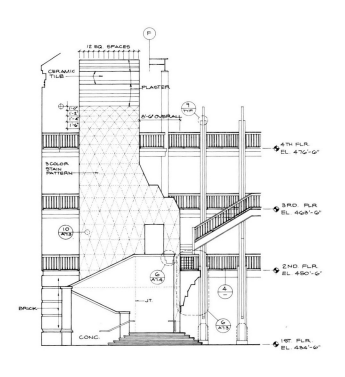

12 EQ. SPACES

CERAMIC
TILE

PLASTER

8'-6" OVERALL

4TH FLR.
EL. 476'-6"

3 COLOR
STAIN
PATTERN

3RD. FLR.
EL. 463'-6"

2ND. FLR.
EL. 450'-6"

BRICK

JT.

1ST. FLR.
EL. 434'-6"

CONC.

The existing chemistry building facade forms one side of the new atrium, while the facade of Willamette Hall creates a new street edge.

On a beautifully landscaped site in San Antonio, a new 45,000-square-foot art college is sited to relate to an existing Spanish Colonial museum and a small community art school. In order to create a sense of community and campus, Moore Ruble Yudell organized the building around a series of courts and streets. A public pedestrian street is lined with a cafe, bookstore, gallery, auditorium, and library. A more private street and court allow for student gathering, work, and recreation. The two streets intersect at a large pavilion. This area serves as the main entrance to the school as well as a reception and celebration space for the auditorium, gallery, and cafe.

In the interest of clear organization, as well as economy, the budget for rich detailing is focused on entry areas and public rooms, while studios and classrooms are simple north-facing loft spaces. Many spaces are designed to accommodate multiple uses: the sculpture courtyard is terraced so that it can also serve as an informal amphitheater; the pavilion court can accommodate special parties and fund-raising activities; library reading rooms are shaped to double as special seminar rooms.

SAN ANTONIO ART INSTITUTE

San Antonio, Texas

During the course of preliminary design, the institute's board was involved in workshops to explore its goals and images. These sessions were important in developing unified goals throughout the design process.

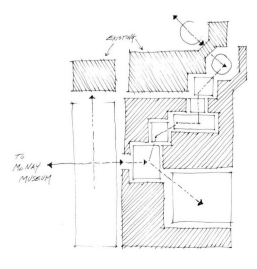

The new building is configured to connect to existing elements and create a sequence of inhabited courtyards.

0 30' 120'

N

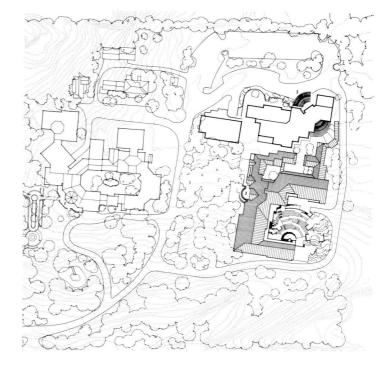

Site Plan

1. McNay Museum
2. Existing art facility
3. New Art Institute

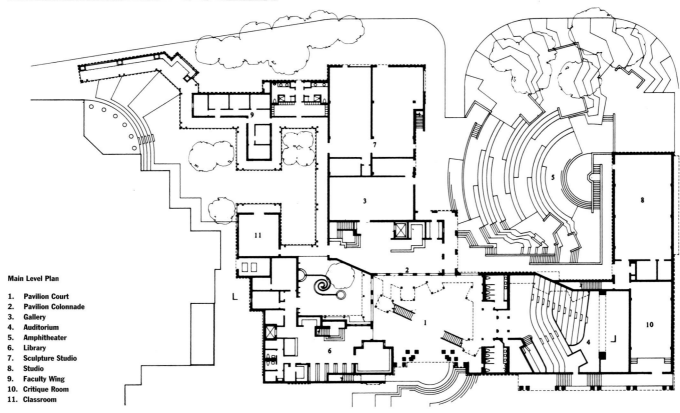

Main Level Plan

1. Pavilion Court
2. Pavilion Colonnade
3. Gallery
4. Auditorium
5. Amphitheater
6. Library
7. Sculpture Studio
8. Studio
9. Faculty Wing
10. Critique Room
11. Classroom

The lively public entrance contrasts with the simpler courtyards within.

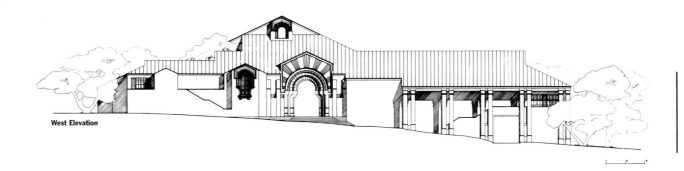
West Elevation

Section A–A

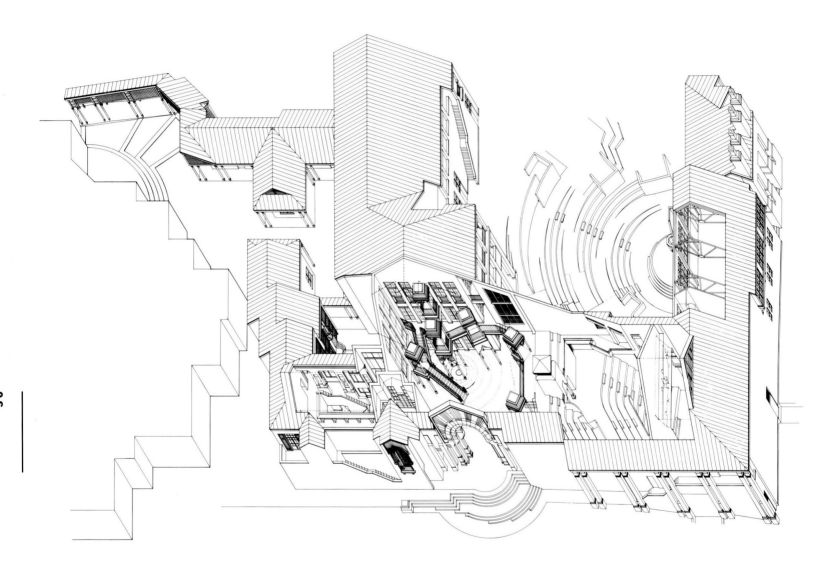

Exterior and interior spaces create a rich spatial sequence.

The sculptural court evokes the Texas vernacular.

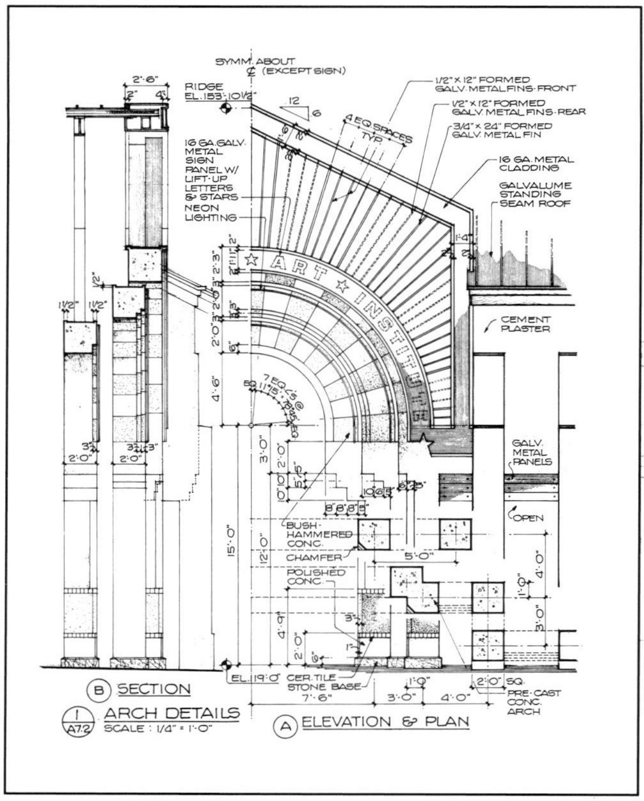

SYMM. ABOUT ℄ (EXCEPT SIGN)

RIDGE EL. 153'-10½"

1/2" X 12" FORMED GALV. METAL FINS-FRONT

1/2" X 12" FORMED GALV. METAL FINS-REAR

3/4" X 24" FORMED GALV. METAL FIN

4 EQ. SPACES TYP.

16 GA. METAL CLADDING

GALVALUME STANDING SEAM ROOF

16 GA. GALV. METAL SIGN PANEL W/ LIFT-UP LETTERS & STARS NEON LIGHTING

CEMENT PLASTER

GALV. METAL PANELS

OPEN

BUSH-HAMMERED CONC.

CHAMFER

POLISHED CONC.

CER. TILE STONE BASE

PRE-CAST CONC. ARCH

SQ.

EL. 19'-0"

B SECTION

1 / A72 ARCH DETAILS SCALE: 1/4" = 1'-0"

A ELEVATION & PLAN

DECOMPOSED GRANITE

CONC

LINE OF ROOF ABOVE

SMOOTH FINISH CONC BORDER

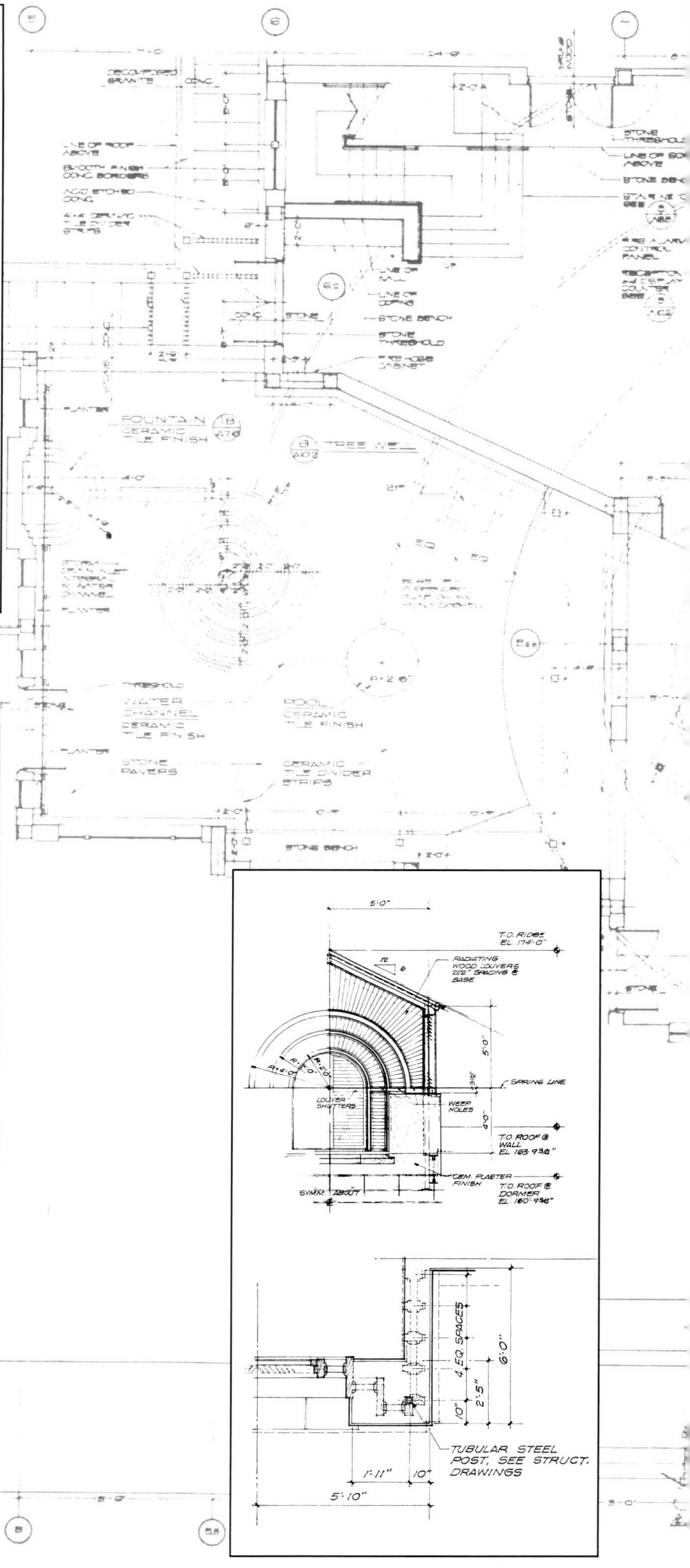

ACID ETCHED CONC

4 X 4 CERAMIC TILE DIVIDER STRIPS

LINE OF WALL

LINE OF COPING

6" STONE BENCH

STONE THRESHOLD

FIRE ALARM CONTROL PANEL

STONE BENCH

STONE THRESHOLD

FOUNTAIN B

TREE WELL

PLANTER

WATER CHANNEL CERAMIC TILE FINISH

POOL CERAMIC TILE FINISH

STONE PAVERS

CERAMIC TILE DIVIDER STRIPS

STONE BENCH

5'-0"

T.O. RIDGE EL. 174'-0"

RADIATING WOOD LOUVERS 2½" SPACING @ BASE

SPRING LINE

WEEP HOLES

LOUVER SHUTTERS

T.O. ROOF @ WALL EL. 163'-9¾"

CEM. PLASTER FINISH

SYMM. ABOUT ℄

T.O. ROOF @ DORMER EL. 160'-9¾"

4 EQ. SPACES

6'-0"

TUBULAR STEEL POST, SEE STRUCT. DRAWINGS

5'-10"

SAN ANTONIO ★ ART ★ INSTITUTE

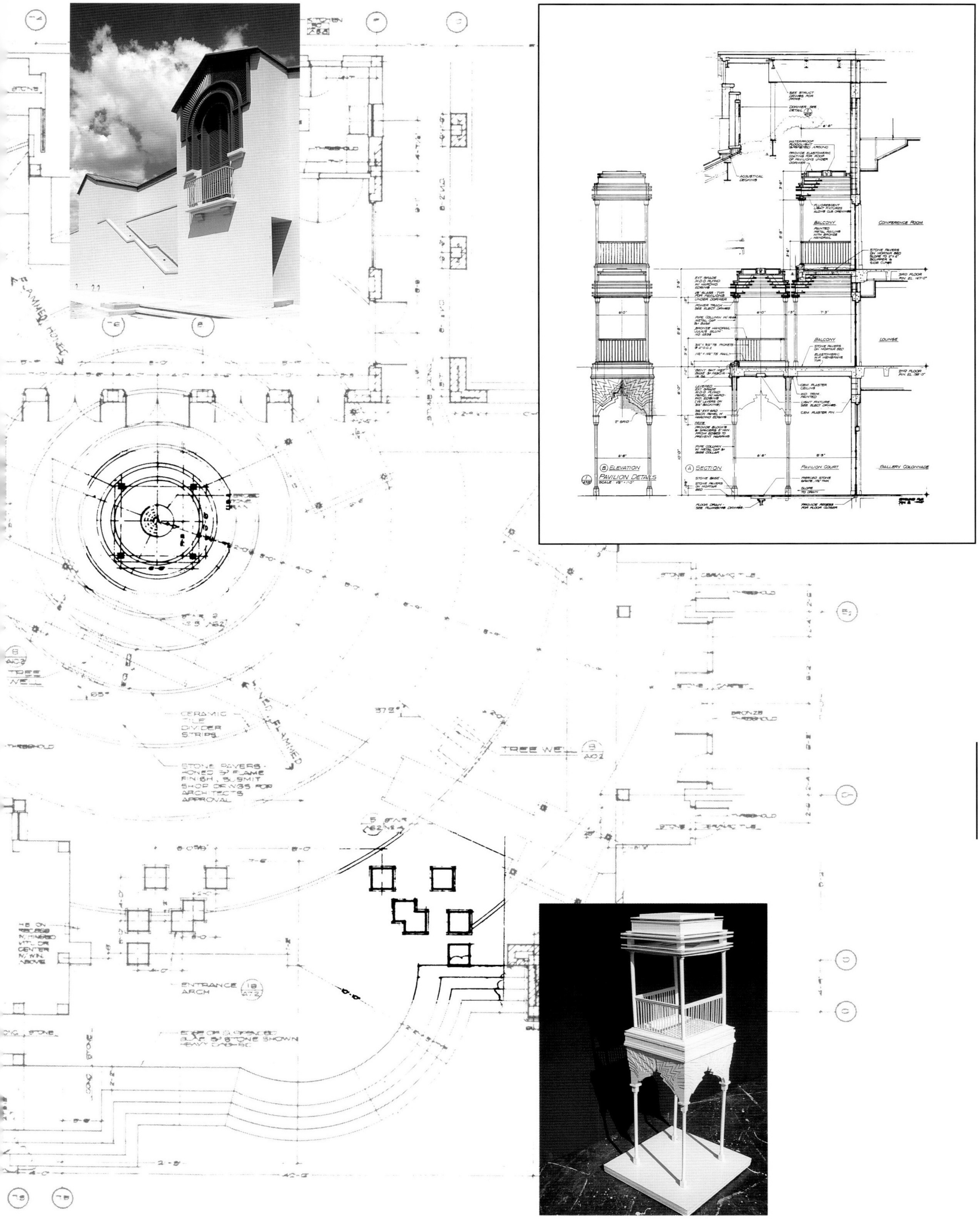
CERAMIC
TILE
DIVIDER
STRIPS
ENTRANCE
ARCH
TREE WELL
ELEVATION
PAVILION DETAILS
SECTION
BALCONY
CONFERENCE ROOM
LOUNGE
PAVILION COURT
GALLERY COLONNADE

This branch library represents the first phase of the Cultural Center for the Tegel Harbor Master Plan. Its construction, started in 1986, coincided with the creation of a large water area adjacent to the harbor, plus a waterfront promenade and 350 units of housing.

The library forms one edge of the Cultural Center: its long hall continues the axis of the harbor along the north boundary of the site, with a view from the main reading room across a forested landscape.

The carefully proportioned industrial loft became the prototype for the library. Its Classical facade is broken by a glassy entrance bay, framed by a pair of free-standing portals. The entry leads to a central rotunda encircled by an arcaded balcony at the second level. From the rotunda, a grand wall of books meanders along one side of the main reading room and gives access to the open stacks and smaller reading alcoves beyond. Passing continuously above the various areas of the loft is a double-layered, vaulted ceiling lit by a clerestory window, which throws light around and through the lower

HUMBOLDT BIBLIOTHEK

Berlin, Germany

vault. On the north side, the light is balanced by a series of bay windows and doors that alternate with niches for books.

The steel and concrete frame is exposed on the interior, and this industrial toughness is elaborated into a playful set of details for arches and ceiling. The book wall itself is, like furniture, composed of painted and natural hardwood. Exterior materials—metal sash, stucco, and the standing-seam zinc roof—combine with spare Classical elements of pre-cast concrete.

Tegel's gently curving harbor edge is re-stated in the plan of Humboldt Library.

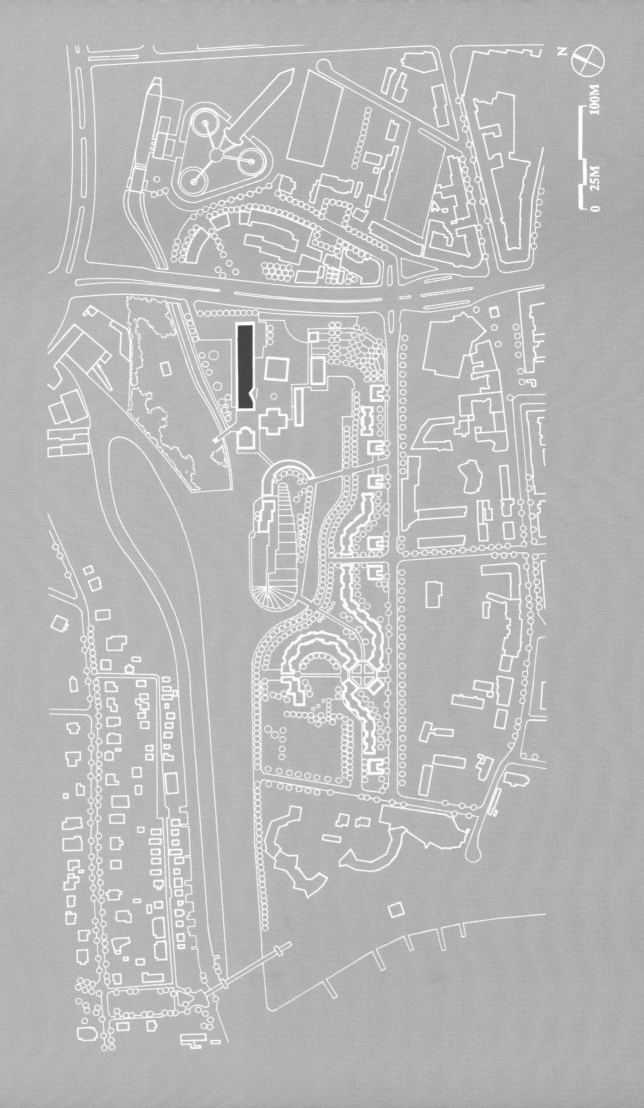

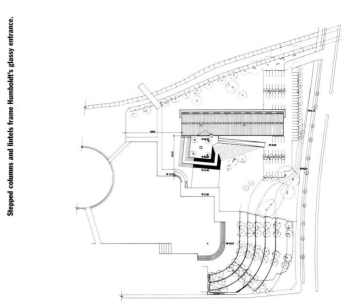

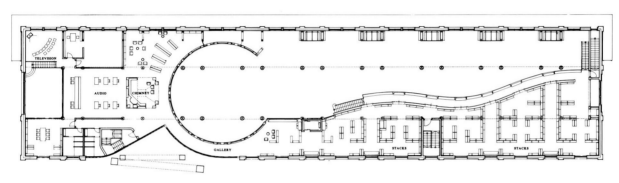

Second level plan

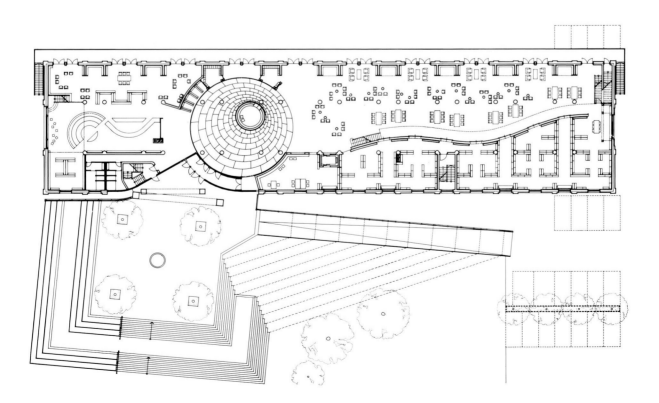

First level plan

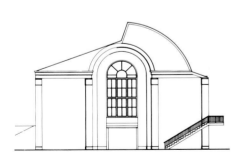

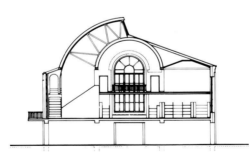

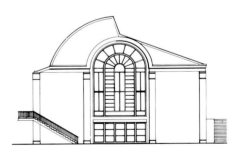

East elevation

Section

West elevation

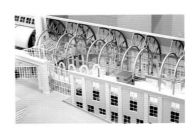

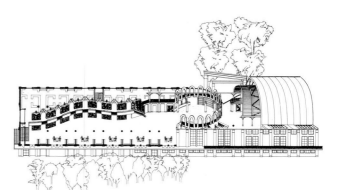

The library continues the axis of the harbor.

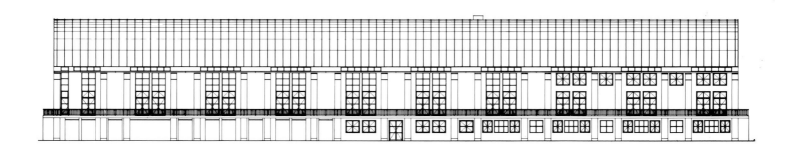

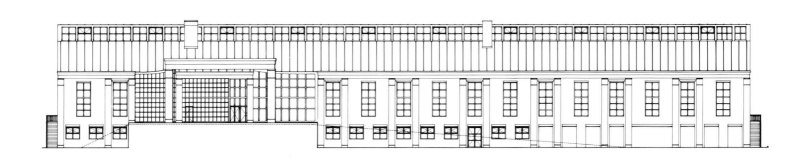

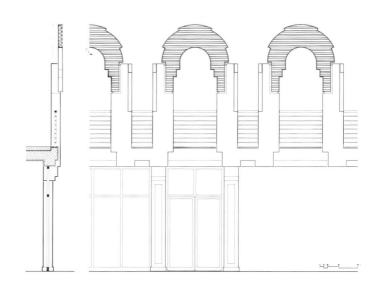

Clerestory light filters through a double barrel vault.

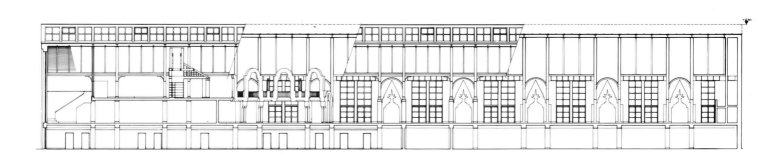

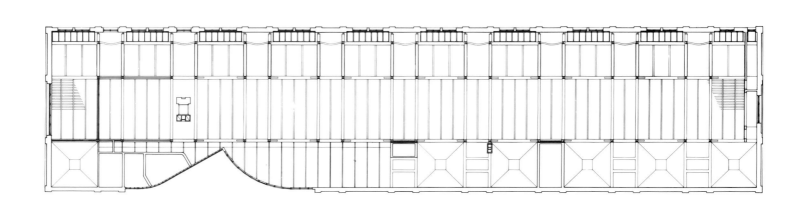

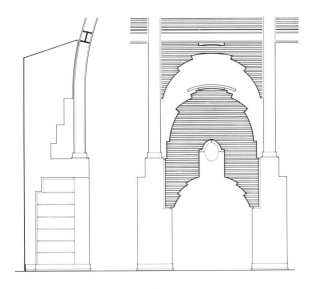

Seating varies from open tables to niches by windows or the fireplace.

The Crossroads School, a lively and progressive secondary school, asked Moore Ruble Yudell to convert a simple concrete warehouse building into a new facility for the visual and performing arts. The campus is located in a dense, largely industrial urban neighborhood.

In the context of warehouse buildings, the facades of the Arts Education Centre create a complementary tough elegance. Cornice and base are established with pre-cast concrete and colored plaster. A light monitor articulates the interior as it meets the sky, giving the building the verticality to strengthen its presence from the campus and beyond.

The campus comprises a row of former commercial and warehouse structures fronting a public street, with a common alley behind. The alley is the spine of the campus, a private pedestrian street that serves as the hub of campus gathering. To give the building an identity on the street for public events, as well as one on the alley, two entrances are connected by a long internal plaza that celebrates the daily interaction of the students and the arts. Dance, art, and music studios have

52 PETER BOXENBAUM ARTS EDUCATION CENTRE, CROSSROADS SCHOOL

Santa Monica, California

windows and addresses along this internal street. The second floor gallery can be opened onto the space, allowing exhibitions the advantage of a larger, unified area, or can be closed off for smaller shows and security. The space is animated by a grand stairway, punctuated with small landings that create "traffic eddies" as the community flows through. The stair and plaza provide places for events and performances, places to see and be seen. Since the opening of the Boxenbaum Centre, the plaza has become the school's major celebration area.

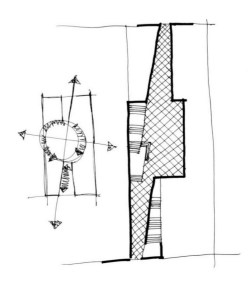

A street, an atrium, and two stairways form the edges along which social activity is fostered.

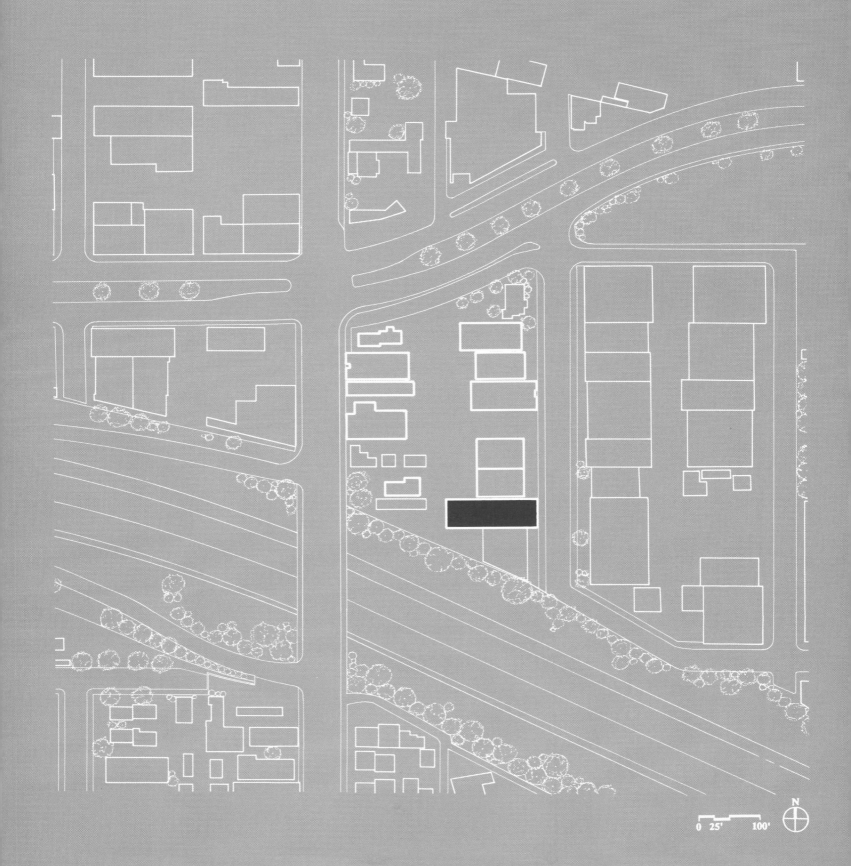

N

0 25' 100'

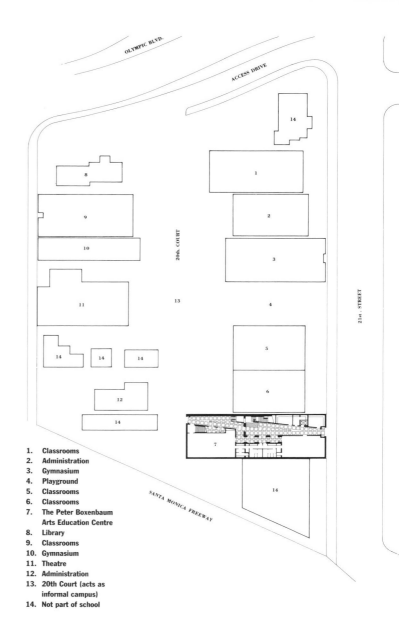

1. Classrooms
2. Administration
3. Gymnasium
4. Playground
5. Classrooms
6. Classrooms
7. The Peter Boxenbaum
   Arts Education Centre
8. Library
9. Classrooms
10. Gymnasium
11. Theatre
12. Administration
13. 20th Court (acts as
    informal campus)
14. Not part of school

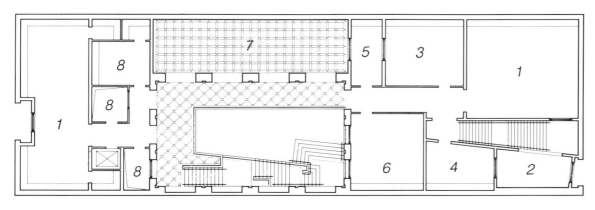

Second Floor Plan

1. Art studio
2. Open to below
3. Art history
4. Seminar
5. Projection
6. Classroom
7. Art gallery
8. Music practice

First Floor Plan

1. Street
2. Court
3. Dance studio
4. Office
5. Storage
6. Electronic music
7. Lockers

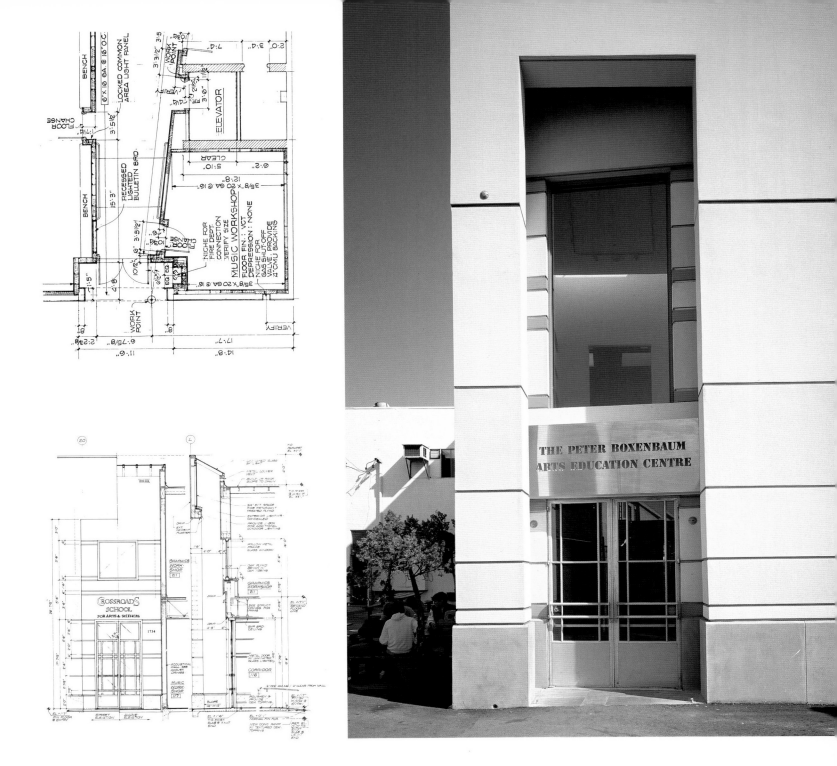

The secondary stairway and campus entrance are skylit.

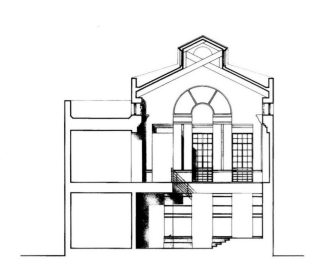

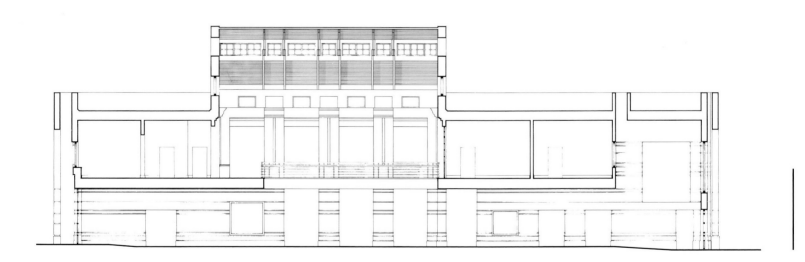

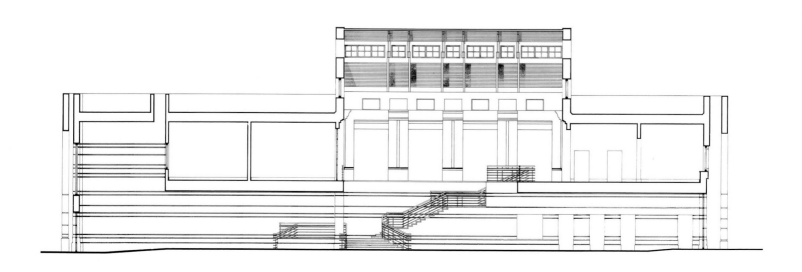

Clerestory light fills the central space.

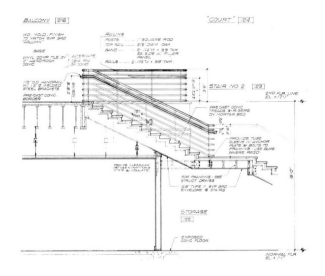

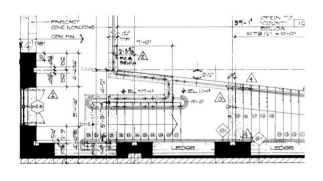

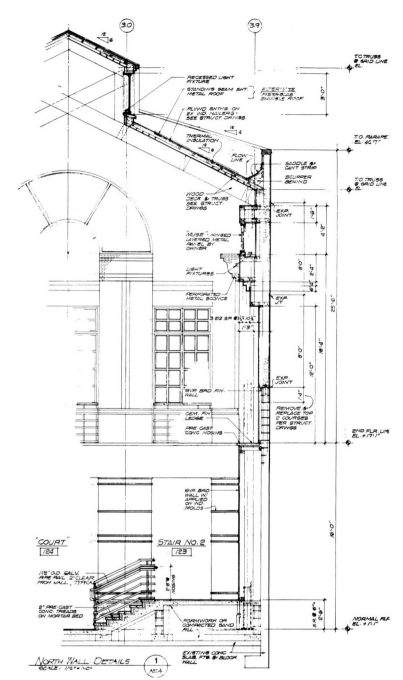

NORTH WALL DETAILS

SCALE: 1/2" = 1'-0"

A grand stairway enlivens the piazza.

This laboratory was financed through an occupancy agreement with a non-profit research institution. The owner and scientists wanted buildings as internally open as possible, with a variety of places for spontaneous meetings, which are the center of their approach to science. Equally important were the qualities of natural light in the labs, a sense of the landscape, and distant views.

The 68,000-square-foot West Wing building attaches to an existing Unit I via a bridge that also contains offices. Below are animal facilities and other equipment shared by the two buildings. Relating carefully to the original project, the West Wing's much larger typical floor area (18,000 square feet) is centered on an intimate court, which is grandly shaded by a trellis and four colossal columns. This court, attended by a small "tower" of conference rooms and animated by a grand stairway, is the social heart of the laboratory. Functionally, the labs are supported and connected by a central equipment corridor plus a spine of special-use rooms. On the exterior, concrete block walls and towers anchor the long, open galleries of the laboratories. On the west side, a grove of eucalyptus trees provides a shady background.

UCSD CELLULAR AND MOLECULAR MEDICINE EAST & WEST

University of California, San Diego, California

To the east, the more recent East Wing adds 52,000 square feet of research space and encloses a terraced lawn to create a shared campus courtyard. In addition, East Wing lies at the end of a long, axial path that forms a spine of pedestrian circulation across the campus; a tower-like facade offers a campus landmark along this axis. Inside, East Wing features the same open, flexible laboratory space that flanks a core of support areas developed for West Wing, as well as a greater number of offices and meeting rooms. Similar materials and a consistent architectural character unify the projects.

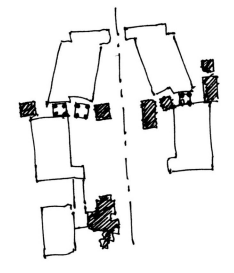

Large lab blocks complement smaller-scaled meeting rooms and terraces.

Reflections on the Project by Rob Wellington Quigley, FAIA

Architect, San Diego, California

The University of California, San Diego campus is admirably sited. Ensconced in a forest of eucalyptus trees on a ridge overlooking the Pacific Ocean, its magnificent setting is second only to that of the University of California, Santa Cruz. Alas, unlike the Santa Cruz campus, UCSD lacked a clear and innovative plan. Even more important, it lacked structure to implement a plan effectively over the long term.

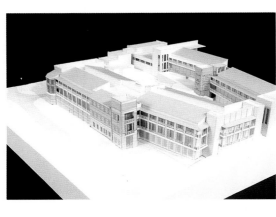

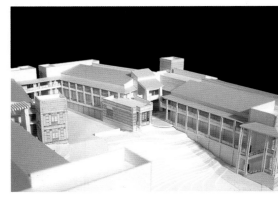

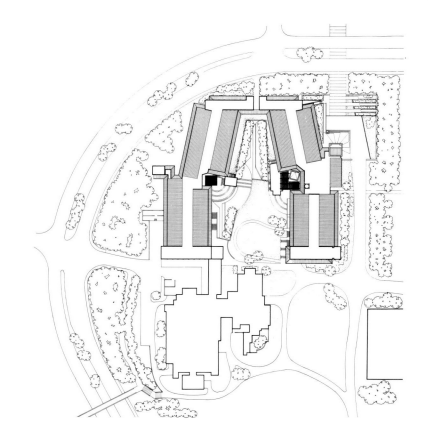

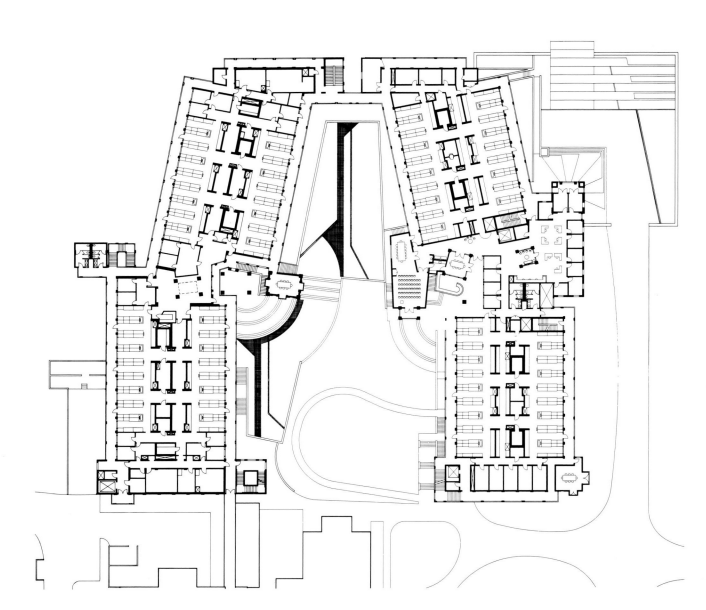

Rather than take advantage of the extraordinary physical opportunities of its site, UCSD slowly squandered its potential over the years. A series of campus plans were partially and half-heartedly implemented. The university's bureaucratic structure favored decisions by internally focused faculty users at the expense of campus architects and planners with broader vision. An ill-conceived design-build program during the 1970s finally drove the larger San Diego community to award the campus an "onion" for poor planning and design.

To its credit, UCSD responded admirably to the wake-up call and, in short order, commissioned a far-reaching and inclusive plan, hired a new campus architect with the ability to implement it, and created a Design Review Board charged with maintaining the long-term integrity of the plan. Although it will take several decades to overcome much of the damage, positive results are already evident. A sense of order and identity is slowly beginning to emerge as architects can now contribute to a larger vision of the place. Moore Ruble Yudell's Molecular Biology Research Facility is one of these contributions. The design significantly addresses a number of campus concerns.

UCSD is lacking in compelling outdoor courts and cloisters. This complex, in contrast, attains a rich and welcome open-space hierarchy from the expansive south lawns to a protected formal garden court and, finally, to delightfully idiosyncratic patios and porches fronting the interior common spaces.

From the larger planning standpoint, the complex becomes a key element in the formation of the "library walk." This important pedestrian mall is a formal axis generated by the central library on the north and anchored by the Moore Ruble Yudell building on the south. Significantly, the complex anchors the mall's southern end while still encouraging people to flow by and beyond to parking and future development to the south. The architecture, despite its Classically inspired "quotes," fits comfortably with the climate and lifestyle of the place. Softly sloping roofs and sweeping verandas provide a relaxed—but purposeful—atmosphere for scientific research.

Conference rooms grouped vertically and horizontally punctuate the courtyard and make points of entry.

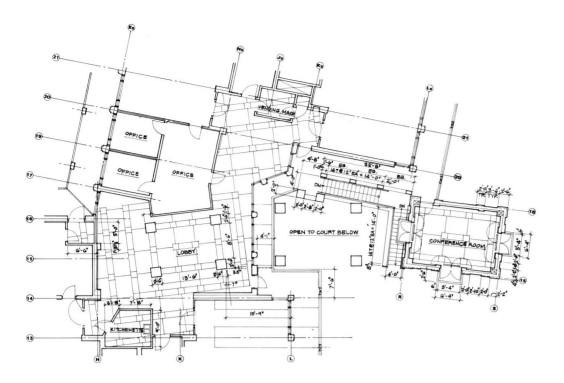

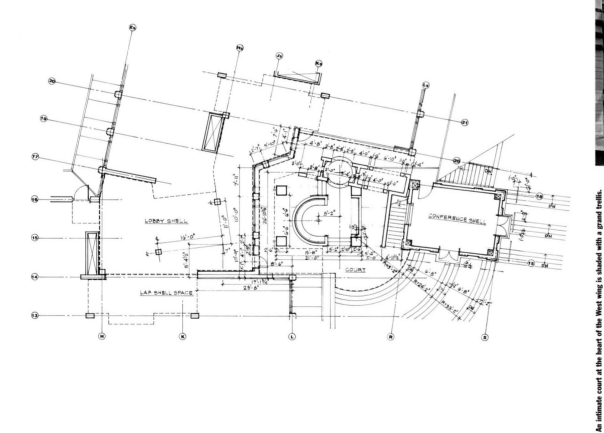

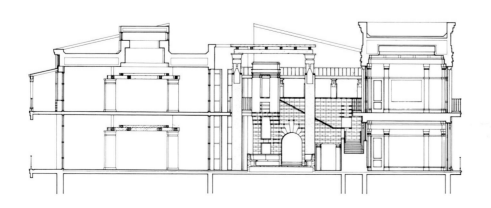

An intimate court at the heart of the West wing is shaded with a grand trellis.

External circulation along open balconies affords researchers daylight and direct views out to the landscape.

A tower of conference rooms marks the entrance to the West wing.

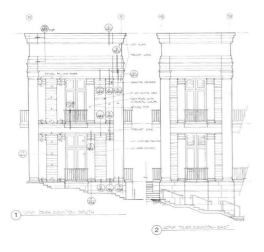

The East Wing also enjoys a trellis-shaded stair and places to gather.

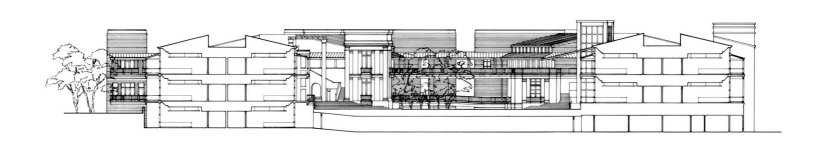

Exterior balconies provide economical circulation as well as sun shading.

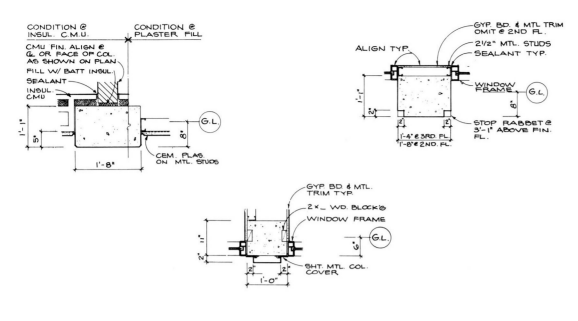

CONDITION @ INSUL. C.M.U.

CONDITION @ PLASTER FILL

CMU FIN. ALIGN @ CL OR FACE OF COL. AS SHOWN ON PLAN

FILL W/ BATT INSUL.

SEALANT

INSUL. CMU

CEM. PLAS. ON MTL. STUDS

1'-1"

5"

8"

1'-8"

G.L.

GYP. BD. & MTL TRIM OMIT @ 2ND FL.

ALIGN TYP.

2½" MTL. STUDS

SEALANT TYP.

WINDOW FRAME

G.L.

STOP RABBET @ 3'-1" ABOVE FIN. FL.

1'-1"

2"

2"

2"

8"

1'-4" @ 3RD. FL.

1'-8" @ 2ND FL.

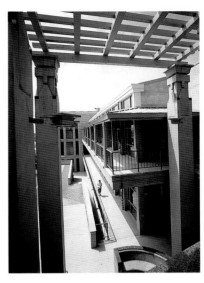

GYP. BD. & MTL. TRIM TYP.

2 x _ WD. BLOCK'G

WINDOW FRAME

SHT. MTL. COL. COVER

1"

2"

2"

2"

6"

1'-0"

G.L.

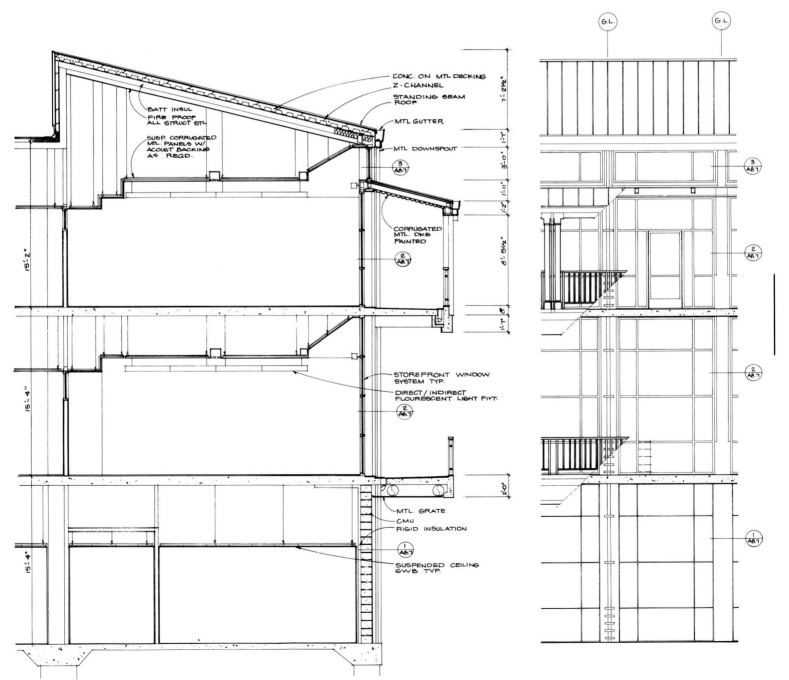

CONC. ON MTL DECKING

Z-CHANNEL

STANDING SEAM ROOF

MTL GUTTER

MTL DOWNSPOUT

BATT INSUL. FIRE PROOF ALL STRUCT STL.

SUSP. CORRUGATED MTL. PANELS W/ ACOUST BACKING AS REQD.

3 / A8.7

CORRUGATED MTL. DK'G PAINTED

2 / A8.7

STOREFRONT WINDOW SYSTEM TYP.

DIRECT / INDIRECT FLOURESCENT LIGHT FIXT.

2 / A8.7

MTL. GRATE

CMU

RIGID INSULATION

1 / A8.7

SUSPENDED CEILING GWB TYP.

15'-2"

15'-4"

15'-4"

7'-2½"

1'-1"

3'-0"

1'-11"

1'-2"

8'-5½"

1'-7"

2'-0"

G.L.

G.L.

3 / A8.7

2 / A8.7

2 / A8.7

1 / A8.7

The Walter A. Haas School of Business Administration is a gateway to its own pleasant courts, plazas, and rooms, from the community into the main campus, and from the growing business community of the West Coast and the Pacific Rim. Designed to encourage interaction, the school is organized around a series of indoor and outdoor spaces that foster informal meetings and accommodate more formal gatherings as well.

The approach from the campus through a large gateway and across a courtyard culminates in the student "forum." This is the heart of the school, a large hall with a great cascade of steps that leads up through the various levels of the hillside site and doubles as seating and overlooks for gatherings, lectures, and performances. Student activity areas, classrooms, and the faculty offices are located adjacent to the forum to insure a critical mass of activity. The other major spaces of the business school—a large lecture hall, the library's main reading room, and a reception hall—surround the forum and reinforce its importance as a crossroads.

WALTER A. HAAS SCHOOL OF BUSINESS ADMINISTRATION

University of California, Berkeley, California

Rapidly changing technology and practice in business education required utmost flexibility in accommodating the school's varied activities. At the same time, the total amount of space required—over 200,000 square feet—presented a challenge: respecting the modest scale of neighboring buildings and the special character of the landscape. Moore Ruble Yudell divided the program into three linked builidngs— a classroom building, a building for offices and research, and a building for support activities including administration, library, and computer center—that are grouped to create a

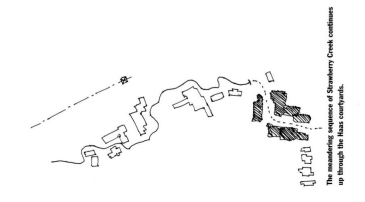

The meandering sequence of Strawberry Creek continues up through the Haas courtyards.

Reflections on the Project by Diane Favro

Associate Professor, School of the Arts and Architecture, University of California, Los Angeles;

editor and contributor, *Streets, Critical Perspectives on Public Space* (UC Press);

author, *The Urban Image of Augustan Rome* (Cambridge University Press)

In 1901, historian William Carey Jones argued that the best way to entice men of wealth to donate money for new buildings at the University of California was to demonstrate that projects bearing their names would be "part of a superb architectural pile that would excite the admiration of the world." Insecure in their cultural and commercial identity, Californians at the turn of the century sought admiration through conformity. The movers and shakers behind the university commissioned John Galen Howard—a conservative East Coast architect—to create a world-class campus in the established, universalized Neoclassical style. Regional design solutions, such as those championed by Bay Area architect Bernard Maybeck in the Faculty Club (1902), were too déclassé, too bohemian, too provincial to represent the state's aspirations.

Today, Californians radiate self-confidence and awareness. An overt symbol of this self-assurance at UC Berkeley is the new Walter A. Haas School of Business. The project is confident not only in size (over 200,000 square feet) and cost ($55 million from private donations), but also in its overt regionalism. The selection of Moore Ruble Yudell is an affirmation of the state's values and identity. Creativity and individualism are mantras of Californians. While a few projects by Moore Ruble Yudell demonstrate creativity in excess, the Haas Business School is an example of the firm in top form, providing history and humanity shorn of Post-Modern frivolity. The building is a mature example of the firm's work: confident in its reverential bows to the early, picturesque Shingle-style architecture of the region, and expert in its handling of contemporary materials, functions, and meanings.

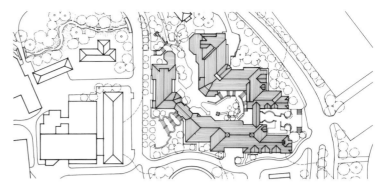

Site Plan

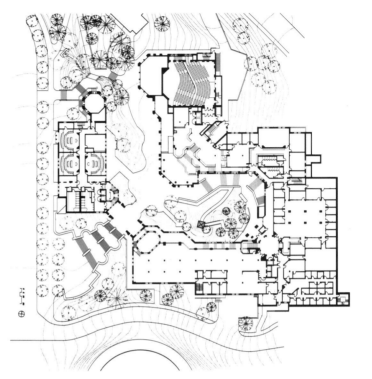

Forum-level Plan

series of outdoor courts and plazas. From a formal entrance court on Gayley Avenue to a sloping glade that flows into adjacent Strawberry Creek, these outdoor places are shaped by buildings nestled into the hillside. Along Gayley Avenue the large complex steps out to the street in two-story wings that are consistent in scale with neighboring residential structures. An arch bridging these wings to link the administrative and faculty buildings frames a view to the university's landmark campanile.

The project's architectural character responds to the Bay Region tradition of the Berkeley campus—the informally planned, carefully detailed wood construction exemplified by Maybeck's Faculty Club and John Galen Howard's Women's Faculty Club. Seismic codes indicated poured-in-place concrete construction; the concrete, left unclad, is formed and painted to evoke the solidity of a rusticated base and the finer grain of Bay Region detailing above. The strong color palette, drawing on regional redwood groves, reinforces the references to this tradition.

Gayley Entrance-level Plan

The experiential richness of the Bay Area environment evokes response and fosters community. Known as much for creating *places* as buildings, Moore Ruble Yudell thrives in this context. In form, the Haas building recalls a rambling English manor house warmed with colors selected by Tina Beebe, in the muted palette of nearby redwoods. The steep roof, animated with gables and bays, echoes the forested mountains directly to the east. Though large, the Business School complex is neither intimidating nor massive. From the residential scale of the two- and three-storied elevation on Gayley Avenue, the building cascades down the hill, accommodating a total of six levels. Its size is mitigated by fracturing the masses into informally arranged groups. Composed of three large blocks organized around a generous courtyard, the structure has the appeal and complexity of a rambling, medieval village. The central open space is both a circulation spine and an outdoor room enlivened with pathways, benches, stairs, and landscaping. On both the east and west, the courtyard is entered through broad Classical, almost Romanesque, arches, establishing alliances with the historical buildings on campus. Like the portal of a city, the proud arch on Gayley Avenue serves as the eastern gateway to the entire campus.

Movement through the Haas building is well-choreographed, sparked with moments of whimsy and engagement. Stairs have long been the forte of Moore and his firm, and this hillside site requires many of them. Here they are treated as sculptural opportunities and meeting points. The communal heart of the building is a lofty internal plaza dubbed the "forum." Stairs ebbing and flowing around terraces provide access to different levels and serve as seating during events. Though grand, the space is humane, enlivened by continuous circulation and other staples of plaza life, including the cafe and mail services.

Subtle design transformations also humanize the large auditorium; an asymmetrical cut in the seating allows for smaller, more familiar groupings, while subtly recalling the underlying slope. Throughout the building, built-in wooden seats transform potentially sterile hallways into occasions for serendipitous gathering. Detailing is familiar, yet provocative. In many public areas the stained concrete floors have the sheen and warmth of aged leather. The unorthodox use of historic ornament, characteristic of much work by Moore Ruble Yudell, is manifested here with restrained expertise. The repetition of stylized, Moore-ish brackets for lighting, furniture, and other embellishments brings a comforting cohesiveness to the expansive structure. Windows and doors proliferate, maintaining continuous connections with the outdoors. From the baronial conference room on the top floor of the west wing, visitors access sun-drenched terraces (unfortunately an addition to the adjacent structure on the west blocked many views to the Bay).

Secure in their identity, Californians of the 1990s do not look to a foreign past for validation; they find ample inspiration within their own heritage and aspirations. The Haas building expresses regionalism not only in explicit design idioms, but also in its underlying concepts. Both the business and university communities have finally realized that enriched and humane environments foster inventiveness as well as broader interaction. The freely cultivated openness and generosity of this building's design encourage expansive community building. Appropriately, entering through the eastern arch of the Walter A. Haas School of Business, one faces toward the Golden Gate and the enticing possibilities of the Pacific Rim beyond.

Bridges cross gateways to link the Haas School's three buildings.

Through a grand entrance arch, the view opens to meandering courtyards below.

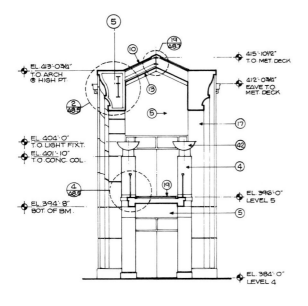

EL. 413'-03/4" T.O. ARCH @ HIGH PT.

415'-101/2" T.O. MET. DECK

412'-03/4" EAVE T.O. MET. DECK

EL. 404'-0" T.O. LIGHT FIXT.

EL. 401'-10" T.O. CONC. COL.

EL. 396'-0" LEVEL 5

EL. 394'-8" BOT. OF BM.

EL. 384'-0" LEVEL 4

WILLIAM F. & JANET CRONK GATE

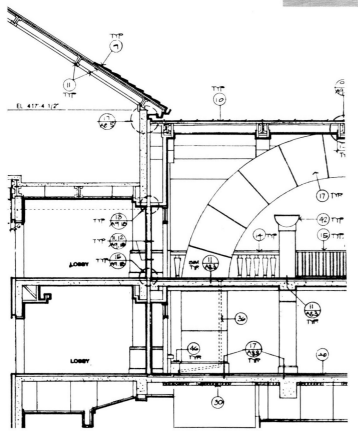

EL 417'-4 1/2"

LOBBY

LOBBY

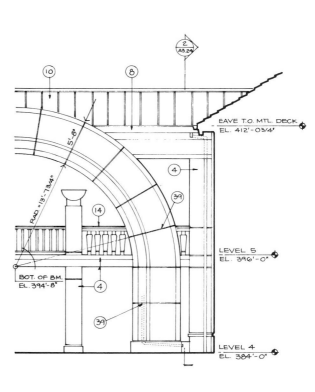

EAVE T.O. MTL. DECK EL. 412'-03/4"

RAD =13'-73/4"

5'-8"

BOT. OF BM. EL. 394'-8"

LEVEL 5 EL. 396'-0"

LEVEL 4 EL. 384'-0"

Interstitial spaces filter daylight into special rooms.

Rich colors and space enliven the classroom wing stair tower.

The California Center for the Arts, Escondido celebrates the arts and more—it creates a focus for a full range of civic habitation. Grouped around the city's Grape Day Park, the Center works carefully with its site and context to create a cultural and civic heart for its rapidly growing community.

The project completes a civic center that includes a recently constructed city hall in a Southern California, Mediterranean idiom, and the city sought architectural consistency with this existing building. Part of the challenge of the project was to achieve an architectural character sympathetic to the new city hall, while interpreting its familiar tradition in a fresh way. At the core of Moore Ruble Yudell's interpretation is an emphasis on the relationship between inside and outside spaces and the development of outside spaces as positively defined outdoor rooms. Another aspect is the play of quiet, understated moments against more active elements at critical points of entry and gathering. Concentrating architectural articulation in this way offers visual punctuation as well as greater economy. Throughout the Center, elements such as towers, special windows, balconies, porches, and arcades play against tranquil

CALIFORNIA CENTER FOR THE ARTS, ESCONDIDO

Escondido, California

walls. This contrast of simple with rich forms heightens the impact of each, while landscape accentuates and enriches this rhythm.

The Center includes four buildings—the 1,524-seat Concert Hall, the 408-seat Theater, the Art Center, and the Conference Center. Conceived as an interdependent whole, the buildings work together to shape more than a dozen courtyards and outdoor spaces of varying size and scale. Exterior and interior spaces are woven together in a carefully composed sequence focused on arrival and movement through the complex, with

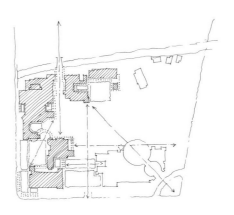

Buildings are configured to shape courtyards and relate to major urban areas.

N

0 40'   160'

landscape playing an integral part in this choreography. The layering of architectural elements also integrates inside and outside. From the innermost performance and support spaces, out through lobbies, arcades, and pergolas, across fountains, courts, and plazas, the eye is drawn from the inside out towards the landscape. These connections emphasize the Center's setting in Grape Day Park.

While working together, each building maintains a distinct character that responds to the particular requirements of its use. The Art Center is a quiet, contemplative place composed of relatively formal, carefully proportioned rooms fronting a quiet garden. A series of north-facing studios is flexible for varied uses; galleries offer differing degrees of daylight, proportions, and sizes for various types of exhibitions. The Conference Center, filled with daylight, offers special meeting rooms, porches, and a breezeway court that link its rooms to the outdoors. The Theater is an intimate 408-seat performance space for events from professional theater and chamber music to community meetings. Placed as a focus of approach from the north parking area, it also forms one flank of the gateway between the arrival court and the park. Its modest lobby is enlivened by a dramatic stair linking the curve of the house inside with the opposing curve of the Center gateway outside.

The Concert Hall, the largest component of the complex, combines the strongest elements of traditional theater configuration with the latest technological advances. All seats are less than 105 feet from the lip of the stage. Back-of-house areas offer access to the outdoors at key points, including private courtyards for actors. Many aspects of the theater are custom-designed, including theater seats and other furniture, as well as extensive lighting inside and outside the house. The Concert Hall lobby spills outdoors in the generous Lyric Court, taking advantage of Escondido's mild climate.

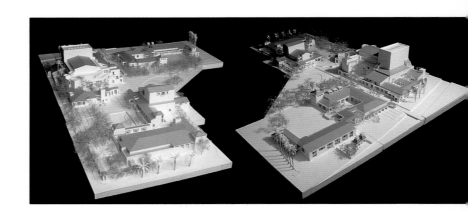

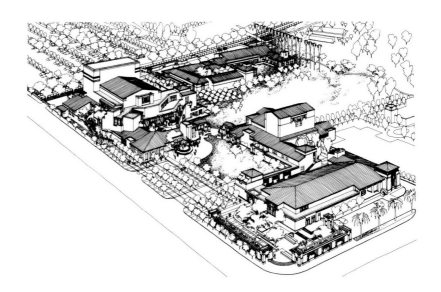

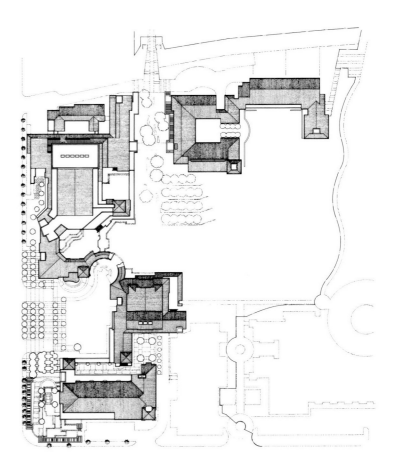

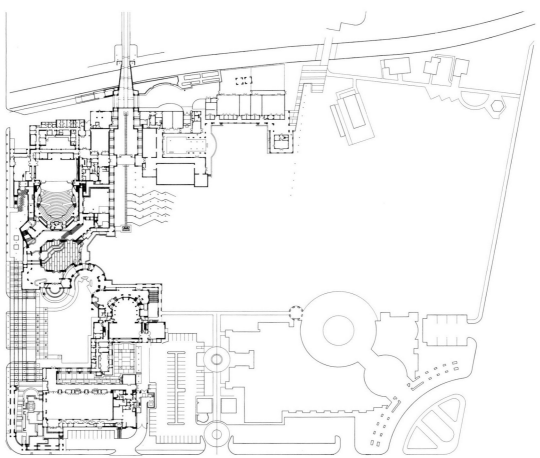

The Lyric Court at the heart of the complex serves as an outdoor lobby to the Concert Hall.

A canopy and box-office tower mark the Concert Hall entrance at the arrival court.

Interwoven geometries create a rich sequence of spaces and views.

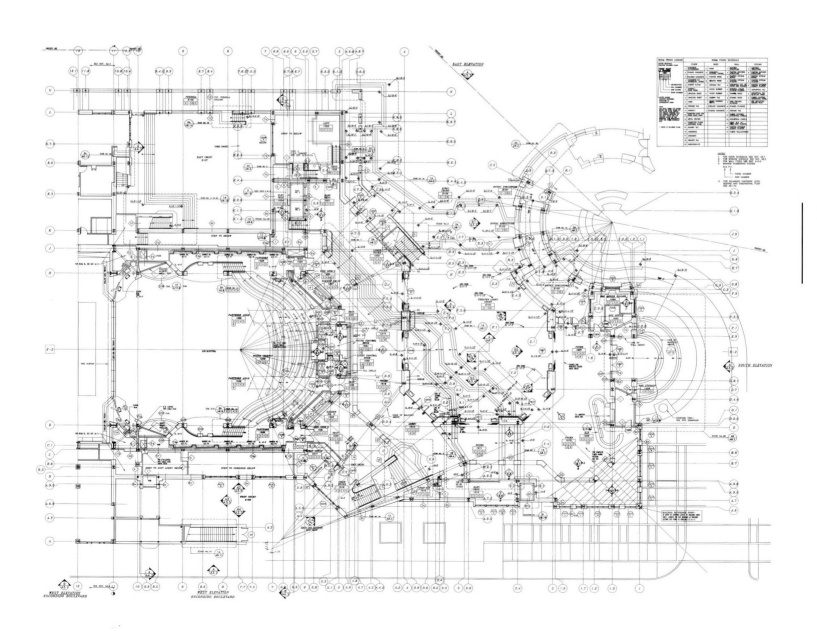

The interior lobby wraps the Lyric Court, punctuated by a grand stair.

Large glass walls slide open to connect the lobby completely to the Lyric Court.

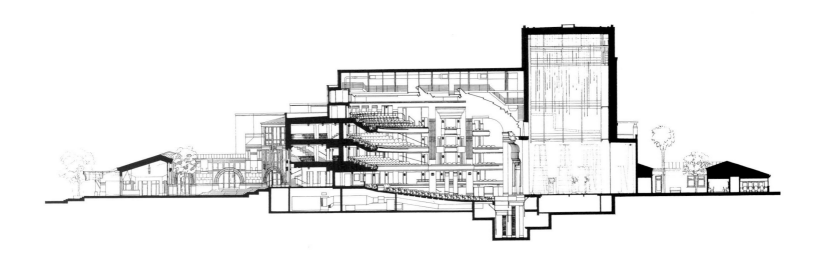

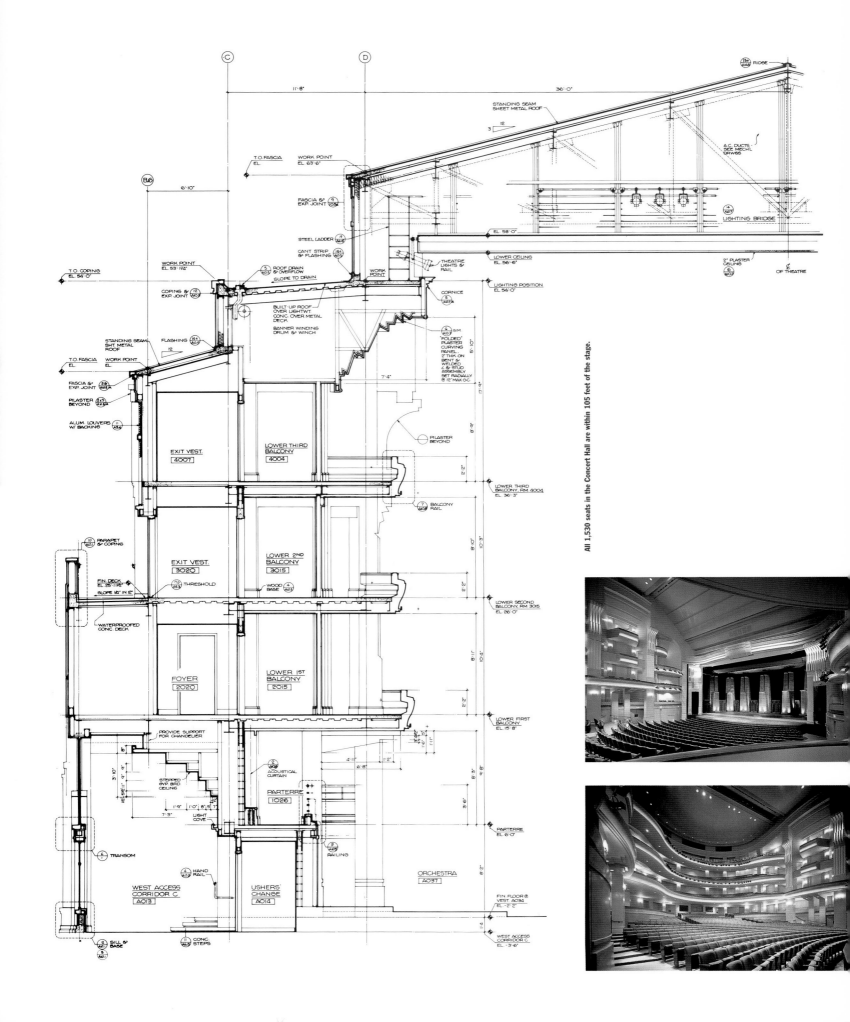

All 1,530 seats in the Concert Hall are within 105 feet of the stage.

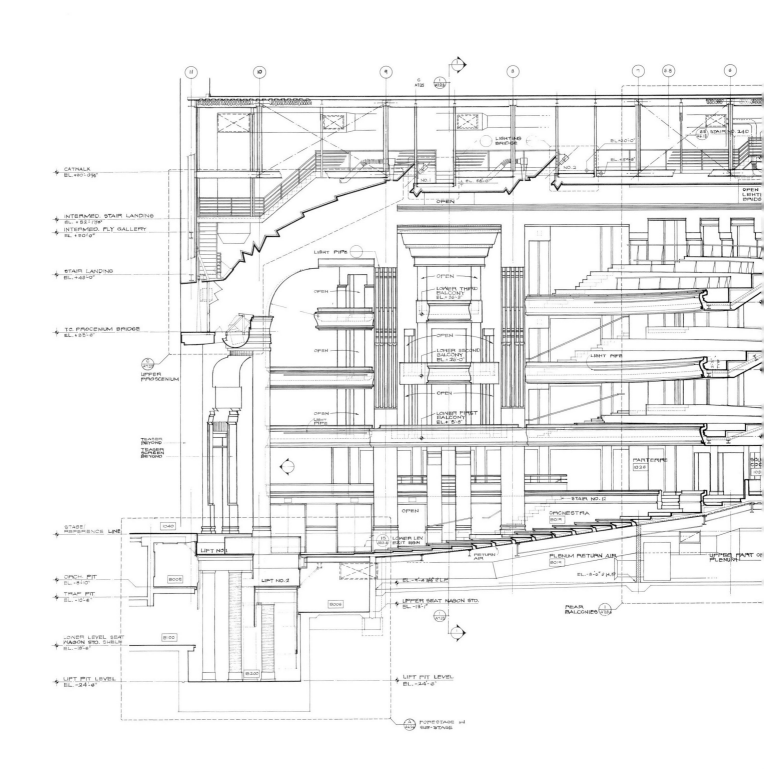

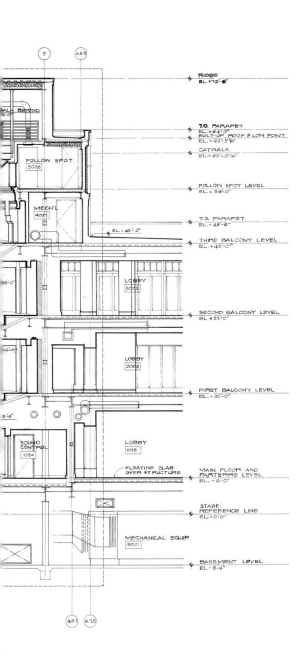

RIDGE
EL. +72'-6"

T.O. PARAPET
EL. +64'-0"
BUILT-UP ROOF @ LOW POINT
EL. +62'-5¼"

CATWALK
EL. +60'-0¼"

FOLLOW SPOT LEVEL
EL. +54'-0"

T.O. PARAPET
EL. +48'-6"

THIRD BALCONY LEVEL
EL. +45'-0"

SECOND BALCONY LEVEL
EL. +33'-0"

FIRST BALCONY LEVEL
EL. +20'-0"

LOBBY
1018

FLOATING SLAB
OVER STRUCTURE

MAIN FLOOR AND
PARTERRE LEVEL
EL. +6'-0"

STAGE/
REFERENCE LINE
EL. +0'-0"

MECHANICAL EQUIP
800

BASEMENT LEVEL
EL. -8'-8"

The Lyric Court is an ideal lobby on Escondido's typically mild evenings.

The Theater's intimate 400-seat house features a full-scale, fully-equipped stage.

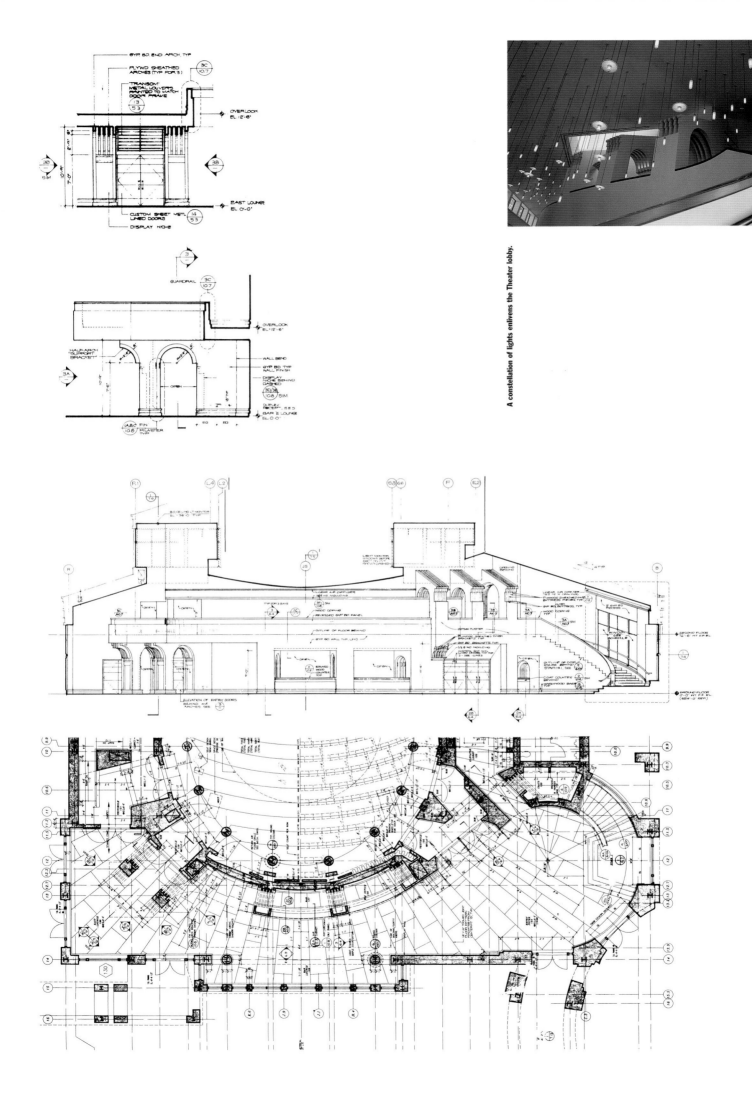

A constellation of lights enlivens the Theater lobby.

The Art Center offers galleries of varied size and proportion.

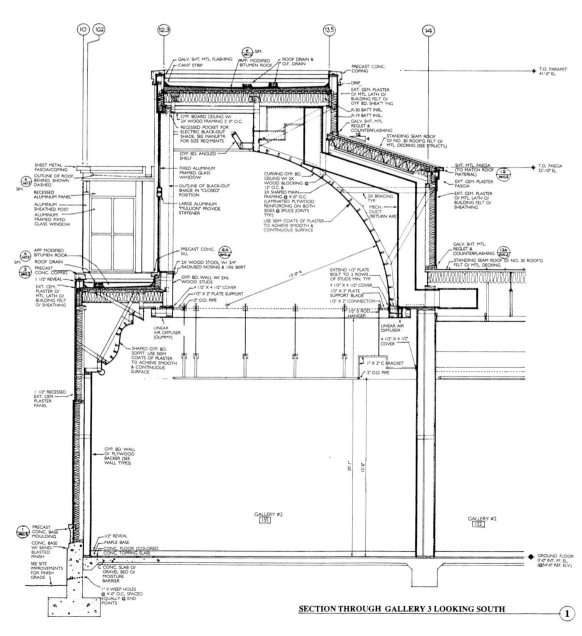

SECTION THROUGH GALLERY 3 LOOKING SOUTH

Sited at the heart of the campus, the University of Washington Chemistry Building must work with a varied set of neighbors. It connects directly to the existing chemistry building, Bagley Hall, the only example of 1930s Art Deco architecture on campus, and relates also to a series of older brick "campus gothic" buildings. It establishes a presence on the Drumheller Fountain Quadrangle, which lies along Rainier Vista—a grand sequence of linked open spaces with an axial view of distant, majestic Mount Rainier. This building also fits carefully into the site's extraordinary landscape: an important grove of Douglas fir that defines an edge of Rainier Vista; a beloved medicinal herb garden thought to be one of the nation's oldest; and a highly traveled pedestrian path, Garfield Lane, which links the central campus to the medical school, with an axial view to Drumheller Fountain.

The massing, plan, and character of the building emerge as a unified, simultaneous response to this complex campus context, the chemistry department's ambitious program, and rigorous technical requirements including more than 200 fume hoods in its teaching and research labs. The massing

UNIVERSITY OF WASHINGTON CHEMISTRY BUILDING

Seattle, Washington

of the building allows the realignment of Garfield Lane without sacrificing its axial fountain view. It groups vertical stacks for the building's fume hoods into exterior "buttresses" to enhance internal flexibility. A "tower" of faculty suites forms a corner of the Drumheller Fountain Quadrangle, while locating these suites conveniently near both faculty offices in the existing building and research labs in the new building. Conference rooms and restrooms are stacked at the far end of the building, drawing traffic through the building to encourage informal interaction within the scientific community. Canted halls on

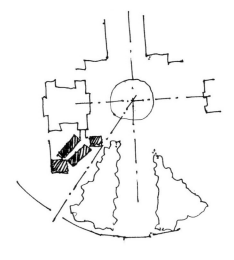

The Chemistry Building moves along a diagonal axis to Drumheller Fountain.

Reflections on the Project by Stephen Harby

Architect, Moore Ruble Yudell

Associate-in-Charge for University of Washington Chemistry Building, Tacoma campus,

and University of California, Berkeley Walter A. Haas School of Business

With no written program, no clear site, and a predetermined architectural vocabulary, the University of Washington asked Moore Ruble Yudell to design an addition to its 50-year-old Chemistry Building. Without an opportunity for unfettered and creative expression, many an architect would have run the other way. But on today's campuses, such commissions are common; indeed, for Moore Ruble Yudell, they are the norm.

each floor increase visibility to all spaces from a central "hinge" at the conjunction of the faculty offices, labs, main stair, and bridge connection to the existing building. This "hinge" also offers views out to Drumheller Fountain.

The architectural character of the building emerges as a response to context, program, and technology. Its subtly patterned brick facing complements the brick of adjacent Bagley Hall. The mass of the building is mitigated by a tripartite division: the more formal faculty tower, with a great degree of openness to the surrounding landscape; the straightforward laboratory bays, with simple industrial sash that recalls Bagley Hall and is punctuated by "buttresses" for vertical ducts; and a simple anchoring volume at the southwest, housing mechanical rooms, air intake, and support facilities such as conference rooms, restrooms, and the elevator.

The first step in the programming and design process was to encourage client and user involvement from the earliest stages. This effort included a series of four participatory design workshops with faculty, students, staff, administrators, and others within and outside the university community. These workshops yielded a basic direction that guided all subsequent design effort; the completed building clearly reflects this early input from the university community.

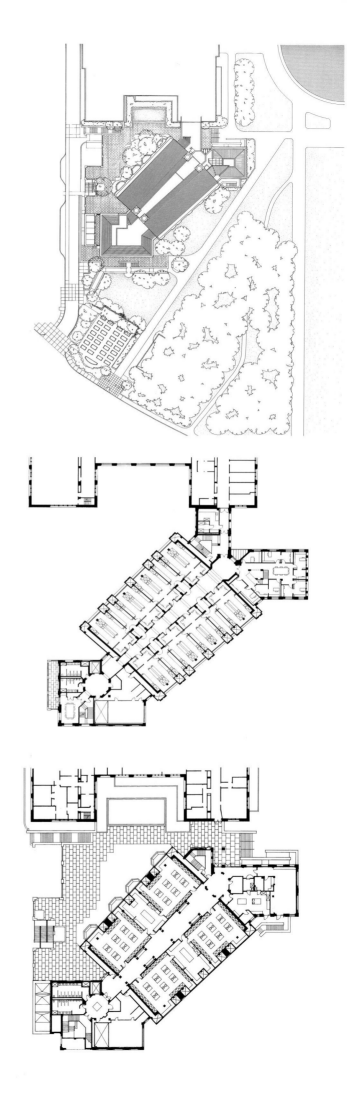

The design of a small, high-tech, industrial complex is what quickly emerged as Moore Ruble Yudell's assignment through an intensive series of participatory workshops. The new building would house both teaching and research laboratories fitted with more than 200 fume hoods, each ducted to the roof. Associated with these labs would be faculty offices, a range of support spaces, and sizable fan rooms supplying the air for the fume hoods. The complex, what then amounted to a giant machine, had to be designed not only to function well for many years, but to take a dignified place on an almost 100-year-old campus. Specifically, the new building could not look industrial, could not seem like an unimportant adjunct to the existing 1930s WPA-built Chemistry Building, and had to foster inter-action among colleagues in the university's scientific community.

The entire planning framework of the University of Washington campus was laid out by Frederick Law Olmsted for the Alaska Yukon Pacific Exposition of 1909 on the same site. While its buildings clearly express the university's early aspirations to East Coast academic traditions, a unique Western stamp was given to the campus by its direct link to the abundant Northwestern natural beauty surrounding the campus. Two important axes on the University of Washington Campus cross the area designated for the new 100,000-square-foot building, and both frame views to the mountains.

In plan, the Chemistry Building is broken into three major components. A pavilion containing the faculty offices occupies the intersection between the new and old buildings: a critical link between the two communities. A three-story bridge allows an important existing pedestrian path to pass between the old and new wings, and stepping forward to frame a view of Mount Rainier, the tower defines the fourth side of the Drumheller Fountain quadrangle. The labs are housed in the second element: a block that is angled to accommodate a stunning grove of mature red-woods to the east and to frame a raised court over the loading dock on the west. The third main element contains support spaces: the fan room, toilets, and seminar rooms. The building's interior was strongly influenced by the desire to introduce natural light into the deep and normally dark laboratories. A splayed corridor with octagonal nodes offers a larger scale to the interior circulation and provides opportunities for departmental gatherings or informal encounters. Interior windows between the labs and the corridor bring additional light and visibility into the labs. Within the tower, offices have been grouped around the perimeter, linked by a sky-lit stair hall and com-mon spaces flooded with natural light.

While the building's exterior pays deference to its neighbors and the strongly traditional campus, characteristic architectural features differentiate each component from the whole. With generous windows, the tower contains clusters of light-filled faculty offices. The lab wing's buttress-like pilasters enclose shafts carrying exhaust air from laboratory fume hoods. Though it resembles others in the quadrangle, the slate roof conceals an extensive network of ducts and fans, betrayed only by four chimneys that emerge from the gable ends.

While we can imagine that, in another 50 years, the Chemistry Building may no longer be on the cutting edge of laboratory design, the design is intended to remain—whether as science labs or even art studios—an integral piece of the whole architectural picture of this campus.

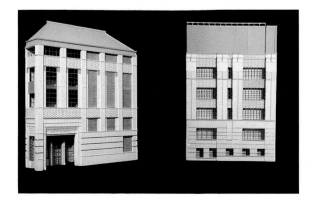

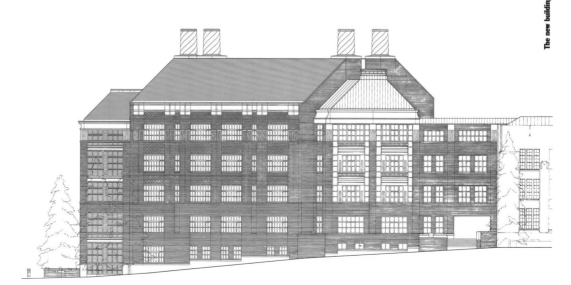

The new building reflects the height, massing and materials of its context.

Executive Vice President, University of Washington

Building on the University of Washington campus, especially in the central area, is not easy. Olmsted plans from early in the century set the basic framework for campus spaces and relationships. Stylistically, the Bebb and Gould Collegiate Gothic tradition makes this campus look like it's 3,000 miles west of where it's supposed to be. Through a combination of skill, luck, and perseverance, the campus has become widely proclaimed, and we proudly and jealously guard it.

At the time we began the project, we had little or no program for the building. We wanted to take the nasty stuff out of our existing 1930s Chemistry Building, but we couldn't afford to renovate it. The Moore Ruble Yudell approach to planning was perfect: Chemistry faculty members spent months rearranging little cereal pieces until "things went together just right" (as Charles would say, in his Goldilocks analogy to architecture).

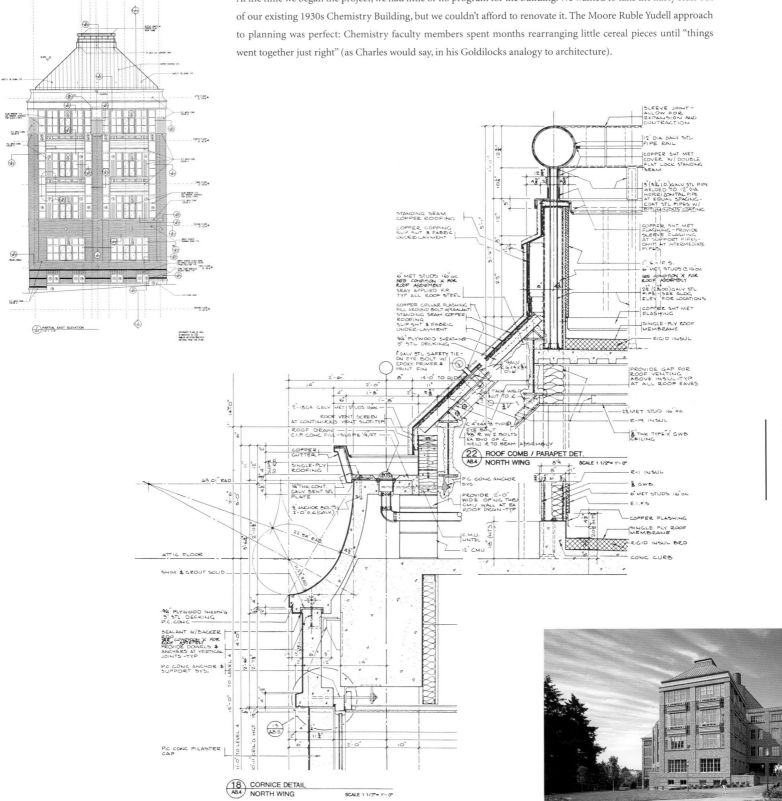

Exhaust from 200 fume hoods is collected into four large "chimneys."

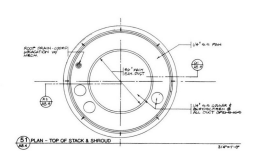

51 PLAN - TOP OF STACK & SHROUD   3/4"=1'-0"

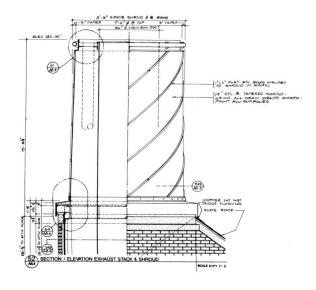

52 SECTION / ELEVATION EXHAUST STACK & SHROUD   SCALE 3/4"=1'-0"

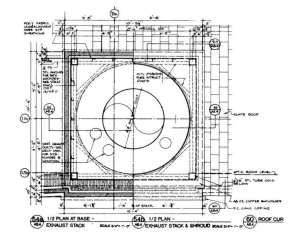

54a 1/2 PLAN AT BASE - EXHAUST STACK   SCALE 3/4"=1'-0"   54b 1/2 PLAN - EXHAUST STACK & SHROUD   SCALE 3/4"=1'-0"   60 ROOF CUR

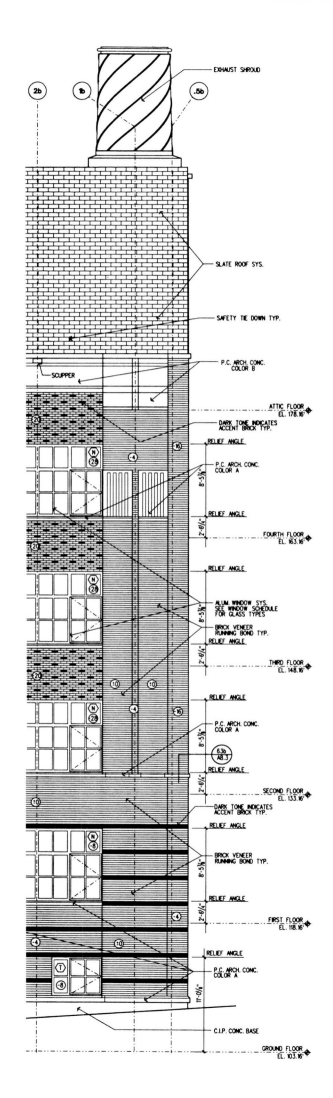

EXHAUST SHROUD

SLATE ROOF SYS.

SAFETY TIE DOWN TYP.

SCUPPER

P.C. ARCH. CONC.
COLOR B

ATTIC FLOOR
EL. 178.16'

DARK TONE INDICATES
ACCENT BRICK TYP.

RELIEF ANGLE

P.C. ARCH. CONC.
COLOR A

RELIEF ANGLE

FOURTH FLOOR
EL. 163.16'

RELIEF ANGLE

ALUM. WINDOW SYS.
SEE WINDOW SCHEDULE
FOR GLASS TYPES

BRICK VENEER
RUNNING BOND TYP.

RELIEF ANGLE

THIRD FLOOR
EL. 148.16'

RELIEF ANGLE

P.C. ARCH. CONC.
COLOR A

RELIEF ANGLE

SECOND FLOOR
EL. 133.16'

DARK TONE INDICATES
ACCENT BRICK TYP.

RELIEF ANGLE

BRICK VENEER
RUNNING BOND TYP.

RELIEF ANGLE

FIRST FLOOR
EL. 118.16'

RELIEF ANGLE

P.C. ARCH. CONC.
COLOR A

C.I.P. CONC. BASE

GROUND FLOOR
EL. 103.16'

A skylit stair in the faculty tower connects all levels of offices.

119

Powell Library, one of UCLA's oldest and most important buildings, needed protection against seismic disturbance, better access for the mobility-impaired, and upgrading of building systems. Moore Ruble Yudell's challenge from the university was to take the need for these improvements as an opportunity, within the limited budget available, to achieve a number of other goals as well: to preserve and enhance the architectural integrity of Powell's historic exterior and important spaces; to create better-organized, more efficient facilities for the various libraries and other functions housed in the building; to make the building easier to move through and to use; to provide for current and future technology demands.

Moore Ruble Yudell's approach was to develop a limited number of strategies for planning and design to address the range of existing problems. For example, the strategy for clarifying Powell's circulation makes the building completely accessible to mobility-impaired persons, and at the same time, more efficient generally.

As the UCLA campus has grown, the south side of Powell Library, originally the "rear" of the building, has come to face

POWELL LIBRARY RENOVATION, UC LOS ANGELES

Los Angeles, California

a large portion of the campus along a major pedestrian spine. In the 1950's, a large addition imposed a blank concrete wall along the south side. To meet current fire and building code regulations this insensitive addition was demolished, providing an opportunity to give Powell an appropriate new south facade and garden courtyard. Materials, proportions, and details are carefully composed to allow the new facade to take its place within the historic building as an appropriate and sensitive—yet fresh—addition.

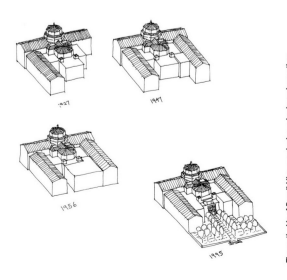

The south side of Powell Library evolved as a haphazard accretion; the renovation clarified the building's order and creates a new south-facing courtyard.

Reflections on the Project by Duke Oakley

Campus Architect, University of California, Los Angeles

The campus of the University of California, Los Angeles presents this generation of architects with a significant urban design problem: to accommodate the increasing density required by the university and, at the same time, enhance the quality of life. This challenge requires that buildings and their resulting external spaces are pleasing as well as useful, that they contribute to the coherence of the overall campus environment, and that the whole, in addition to individual pieces, be of the highest quality. The locus for this exercise in excellence is 420 acres in Westwood with more than 12 million square feet of buildings that compose the UCLA campus.

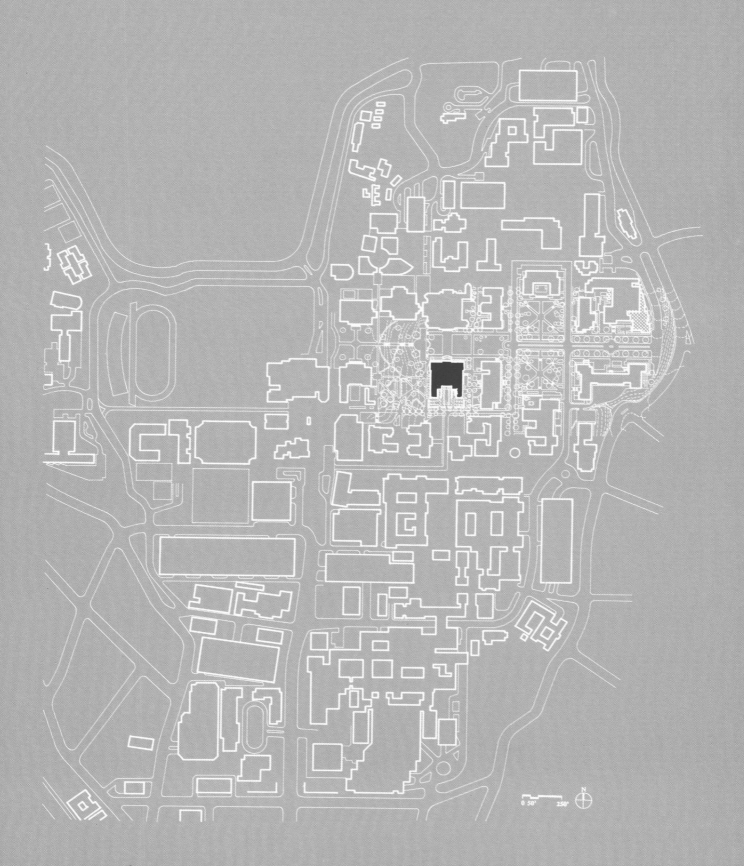

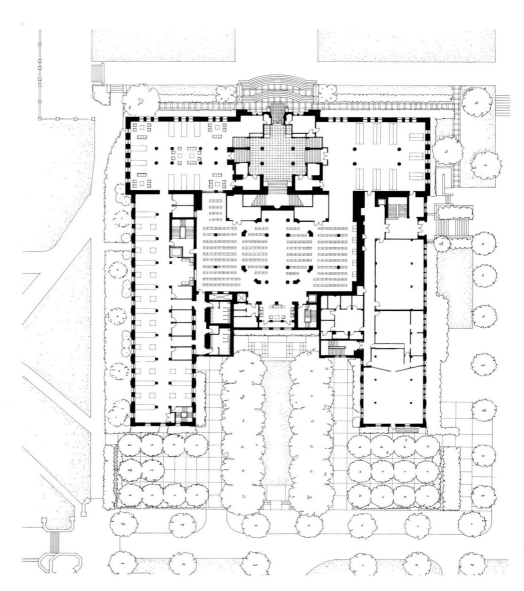

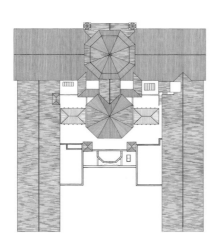

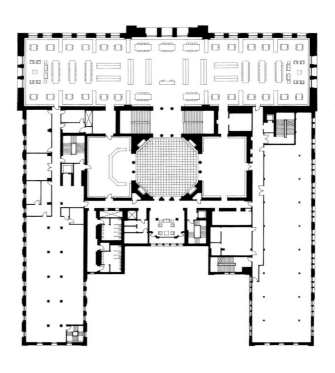

San Francisco architect George Kelham produced the first campus design for UCLA's Westwood site. His 1926 rendering is purely Beaux-Arts: a major east/west axis and a principal cross axis organize buildings around a central open space. To the north of the quadrangle stands a building resembling Powell Library, topped like Powell by an octagonal dome. To the south of the major axis, with but a single tower at the time of the rendering, stands the future Royce Hall. The architectural style of the buildings appears to be Mission—rather than the Romanesque that was actually used—but through the mid-1940s, all later versions of the evolving UCLA campus plan followed the basic organization of this first conception.

Since the 1920s, details of architectural style and specific placement of buildings have determined neither the organizational whole nor the evolving sense of place created at UCLA. Rather, three contributing factors have been responsible for those aspects of the campus that are seen as its best characteristics: the impact of the land itself, the urban design principles of the École des Beaux-Arts, and the particular image of the college campus as it has developed in America.

The terrain, the climate, and the geography of Los Angeles continue to be major forces in physically shaping UCLA. While this surrounding natural context includes such attractive features as a temperate climate and the Pacific Ocean, it also includes other considerably less-appealing aspects, such as the increasing density of West Los Angeles and the potential for earthquakes. The topography, including a filled-in arroyo shown in the foreground of the Kelham rendering spanned by an impressive arcaded bridge, has been an active organizing element of the campus from the first.

Beaux-Arts techniques for organizing and giving form to an accretion of buildings have shown themselves to be particularly effective in generating memorable college and university settings. Informal, so-called "organic" or "picturesque" techniques have failed to remain coherent at any scale larger than an entrance drive, a few core buildings, and playing fields. Alternatively, the abstract physical planning techniques generally espoused by Modernist planners have not aged well; they now seem soulless and often confusing at the pedestrian scale. At UCLA, axial and hierarchical relationships of buildings, building groups, and enclosed outdoor spaces based on Beaux-Arts planning principles have given identity to the developing campus.

Finally, UCLA's campus design has been shaped by the intellectual landscape of the American university: that is, the general concept of college campus shared by its community—faculty, students, and country. As an imageable, coherent entity distinct from its non-academic surroundings, the college campus would appear to have been invented in America. Indeed, according to historian Paul Turner, the modern term "campus" was first used in reference to the lawn in front of Princeton's Nassau Hall. Our images of remembered places and the imagined ideal of an American college campus are not initially dependent on responses to particular geographical sites.

Moore Ruble Yudell is involved with two projects instrumental in re-establishing the integrity of UCLA's overall campus plan—the first of these is the Powell Library project. On the interior, the project reclaims Powell for the next generation of undergraduate library users; on the exterior, the design reasserts the organizing power of the north-south axis. Moore Ruble Yudell's other project is the Hugh and Hazel Darling Law Library Addition, which will emphatically establish the present-day eastern terminus of the campus' main axis at a point very near its original entrance.

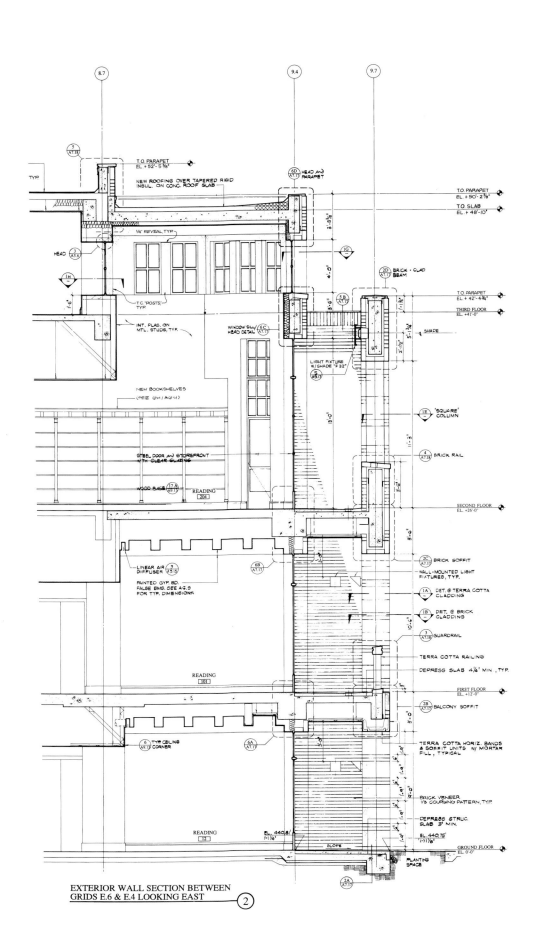

EXTERIOR WALL SECTION BETWEEN
GRIDS E.6 & E.4 LOOKING EAST   (2)

The original rotunda, fully restored.

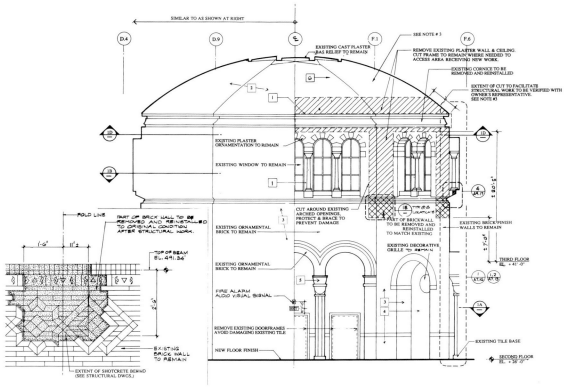

SIMILAR TO AS SHOWN AT RIGHT

SEE NOTE # 3

EXISTING CAST PLASTER
BAS RELIEF TO REMAIN

REMOVE EXISTING PLASTER WALL & CEILING.
CUT FRAME TO REMAIN WHERE NEEDED TO
ACCESS AREA RECEIVING NEW WORK.

EXISTING CORNICE TO BE
REMOVED AND REINSTALLED

EXTENT OF CUT TO FACILITATE
STRUCTURAL WORK TO BE VERIFIED WITH
OWNER'S REPRESENTATIVE.
SEE NOTE #3

EXISTING PLASTER
ORNAMENTATION TO REMAIN

EXISTING WINDOW TO REMAIN

EXISTING BRICK FINISH
WALLS TO REMAIN

FOLD LINE

PART OF BRICK WALL TO BE
REMOVED AND REINSTALLED
TO ORIGINAL CONDITION
AFTER STRUCTURAL WORK.

CUT AROUND EXISTING
ARCHED OPENINGS,
PROTECT & BRACE TO
PREVENT DAMAGE

PART OF BRICKWALL
TO BE REMOVED AND
REINSTALLED
TO MATCH EXISTING

TOP OF BEAM
EL. 491.34'

EXISTING ORNAMENTAL
BRICK TO REMAIN

EXISTING ORNAMENTAL
BRICK TO REMAIN

EXISTING DECORATIVE
GRILLE TO REMAIN

THIRD FLOOR
EL. + 41'-0"

FIRE ALARM
AUDIO VISUAL SIGNAL

EXISTING
BRICK WALL
TO REMAIN

REMOVE EXISTING DOORFRAMES
AVOID DAMAGING EXISTING TILE

EXISTING TILE BASE

NEW FLOOR FINISH

EXTENT OF SHOTCRETE BEHIND
(SEE STRUCTURAL DWGS.)

SECOND FLOOR
EL. + 26'-0"

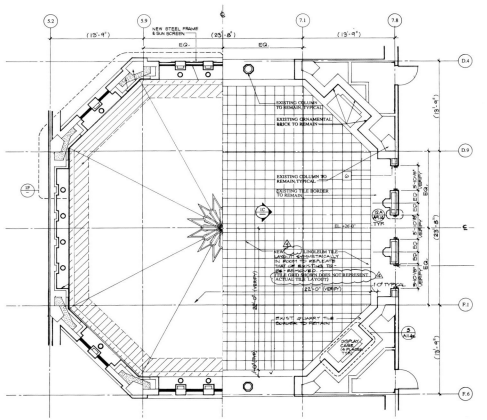

NEW STEEL FRAME
& SUN SCREEN

EQ.   EQ.

EXISTING COLUMN
TO REMAIN, TYPICAL

EXISTING ORNAMENTAL
BRICK TO REMAIN

EXISTING COLUMN TO
REMAIN, TYPICAL

EXISTING TILE BORDER
TO REMAIN

EL. + 26'-0"

NEW LINOLEUM TILE
LAYOUT SYMETRICALLY
IN ROOM TO REPLATE
THAT OF EXISTING TO
BE REMOVED.
(TILE GRID SHOWN DOES NOT REPRESENT
ACTUAL TILE LAYOUT)

EXIST. QUARRY TILE
BORDER TO RETAIN

DISPLAY
CASE
(4 PLACES)
TYP.

ON CAMPUS AND COMMUNITY

THE SHAPE OF COMMUNITY

by Buzz Yudell

ESSAY

Community is a fragile and precious phenomenon. It forms the foundation for our sense of identity and well-being; indeed, it is critical to the survival of our societies. Too often, architects feel powerless in creating places for community. At times we abdicate entirely, ignoring our potential to affect the people who dwell in our buildings.

Perhaps we have been conditioned to feel that social, economic, political, and cultural forces are too powerful or complex to address by way of form- and place-making. But such an attitude undermines the power of architecture and the potency of architects as builders of community and society.

In our work, we have taken much pleasure and solace from the belief that the forms we generate and their underlying ideas can make a significant contribution toward creating that intangible and essential spirit of community. The very skills that form the foundation of our training and talents as architects can be instrumental in this effort: our ability to shape spaces for habitation; our appreciation of a building's power to connect specifically with its site; our sensitivity to the qualities of light and climate that endow a place with unique character; and our understanding of proportion and scale as they relate to our bodies and spirits.

There are innumerable ways of analyzing how an architect can affect people's experience of place. The following five categories have informed our effort to shape community.

SCALES OF HABITATION

Individuals and communities understand and experience their lives at multiple scales simultaneously. Understanding the presence and meaning of these multiple frames of reference is critical to us in the initial planning of a building. We look at the overlapping scales of a place: the region, the locale (city, suburb, countryside), the campus context, the building context, and the building components (such as individual rooms, clusters of rooms, circulation, exterior spaces, and special social spaces at the smallest scale). Each of these scales presents different opportunities for revealing the particularities of a site.

Experiences of varying scales tend to interact in complex ways. For example, a small resting place along a stair or corridor can interact with a large gathering space. Such reciprocities can enhance the richness of community as a collection of diverse individuals and groups. Vernacular architecture and urbanism across virtually all cultures have profound lessons for us in the making of community. Close at hand, the Campground on Martha's Vineyard provides a vivid expression of individuation within a clear whole. Typologically identical cottages are given unique expression by the color and ornamentation of their porches.

The individual and family are clearly "identified" and given an architectural face within the community, expressed at an intimate scale. Like wagons circled for protection, the encircling of a shared common space by these cottages expresses the unity and larger social needs of the whole.

Seven thousand miles to the west, the traditional courtyard houses of urban China embody nesting scales of habitation and social networks. The traditional extended family within an organically growing courtyard complex allows for degrees of individual expression while it literally extends the fabric of the family to the next scale of habitation. The whole, in turn, occupies a clear place within the orthogonal network of the village or city, establishing a clear expression of public entry as distinct from the reticulated network of private spaces.

Seven thousand miles to the east of the Campground, the vernacular villages of the Greek islands represent the built expression of several scales of social interaction. The individual porch and stoop are distinguished by both their sculptural clarity and the colorful ornamentation of doors and gates. The clarity of the street as a communal artery is expressed by the clear delineation of the "street wall" and by its faithful conformity to the topography. At their intersections, the streets link into social nodes and, where they connect at the edge of the harbor, into one grand confluence. The ability to inhabit this range of social scales allows for both choice and a sense of participation in a greater whole.

When we were designing a new science complex for the University of Oregon in Eugene (working with the Ratcliff Architects), there was an intense desire for community. In large part, our job became listening to our clients. A surprising number of buildings on this and other campuses over the past 30 years have, despite their architects' good intentions, created barriers to shaping community. At the University of Oregon, five departments had an extraordinarily

complex social ecology. Each possessed its own strong culture; all had strong social and academic inter-relationships; interaction between students, faculty, and staff were, in turn, very important. The sciences as a whole bore a central relationship to the campus.

Working within the *Pattern Language* of Christopher Alexander that had been adopted for campus planning, we sought to give physical expression to the many scales of habitation that we began to understand, as well as to allow for the development of new levels of interaction yet to be forged. In the new buildings, each department has informal meeting spaces along stairs and halls. Each has a departmental "hearth" and a series of south-facing porches and courtyards appropriate to this northern climate. Departments are loosely linked by the informal "science walk," and more formally connected by interdepartmental bridges where lounges and staff offices occur. The science atrium became a spatial crescendo in which old and new buildings surround a space that links all departments, and it has since become a celebratory room not only for the sciences, but for the campus as a whole.

HIERARCHIES OF DOMAIN

To shape a set of spaces is more than an abstract, geometric exercise. We seek to intensify the gradations from public to private realms in our buildings for institutions. In addressing the related qualities of a sense of ownership or participation in a place, we seek a rich shading of formal hierarchies, avoiding either/or solutions to the complex issue of public versus private space.

The great academic campuses of both Europe and the United States provide exceptional lessons in the subtle overlappings of domain. At Oxford and Cambridge the individuality of each college within the university provides a source of both pride and identity. Within the college, student and faculty apartments provide for diversity of identity within the whole. I have always been particularly taken by the manner in which social custom and physical articulation can aid in the flexible expression of domain. For example, many of the student apartments in the older colleges have two exterior doors. By choosing how to deploy these two social filters—both closed; outer open, inner closed; both ajar, and so on—students can signal, in a commonly understood language, the degree to which they welcome visitors or wish to maintain their privacy.

At the California Institute of Technology, Bertrand Goodhue and Gordon Kaufman extended the tradition of great campus planning. Here we were asked to design the new Avery House as a combination of residential living for students and faculty, and social and seminar space for general campus use. Goodhue's South houses provide extraordinary examples of how the proportions of courtyards and weaving of circulation can create a powerful and particular residential experience. Kaufman's Athenaeum develops a similarly potent expression of the way in which courtyard architecture can enhance collegial dining and seminars.

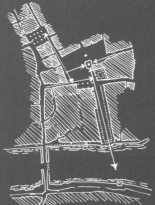

At the Uffizi, a powerful new geometry links the River Arno with the Piazza della Signoria.

Trying not to be daunted by the finesse of these precedents, we sought to explore the subtle qualities of spatial proportions and sequence in developing a place where the shaping of the exterior is as critical as that of the interior. Each courtyard is proportioned relative to a hierarchy of its use and its climatic orientation. Working with landscape architect Pamela Burton, we developed each courtyard as a unique spatial, landscape, and social experience.

Hierarchies of domain are enhanced by the development of what we came to call a "social plaid." We parsed and positioned the student and faculty rooms throughout the building so that every room has multiple realms of identity. Entryways cluster around common stairs and lounges to encourage vertical integration. Bathrooms and kitchens are dispersed horizontally for a second sense of group identity. Each space further identifies with its courtyard and stands as a distinct but related piece of the larger university community. The proportions of spaces, arcaded exterior circulation, and this "social plaid" support multiple scales of habitation and a rich sense of integration within the community.

GEOMETRIES OF CONNECTION

The geometric specificity of our sites provides powerful cues for connecting new buildings to the existing fabric, for fostering a range of social interaction, and for investing new places with particularity and memorability.

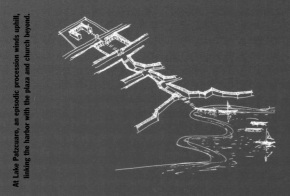

At Lake Patzcuaro, an episodic procession winds uphill, linking the harbor with the plaza and church beyond.

Historically, geometric connections in urban settings have developed as a result of clear design intention, and the shaping of built form by patterns of use over time. Vasari's design for the Uffizi inserts a clear new urban geometry that connects the Piazza della Signoria to the important edge of the River Arno, functioning with equal elegance at the urban and building scale. In the isolated town of Chupicuaro on the edge of Lake Patzcuaro, the church is located on the highest ground adjacent to the town square. An episodic procession uphill links the water's edge (with its connection to other communities) to the town square and church (with their connections to the diurnal and the divine).

Our competition scheme for the University of Maryland Performing Arts center grew out of responses to tensions between the site and program. These issues were resolved, in part, by integrating the diverging geometries of two parts of the campus. This allowed us to make references and spatial connections to two otherwise divided precincts. A third geometry, developed through the bisection of the first two, creates a highly animated, linear social center for the building. This internal street stretches from a formal entry court to an informal amphitheater, and along its length every major performance space presents a strong presence. Together they make a family of buildings along a civic street that is contrapuntal to the geometries of the separate departmental courtyards.

CHOREOGRAPHY OF COMMUNITY

Places that invite a kinesthetic experience of space heighten one's involvement with both the place and other inhabitants. The "fit" between the building and the inhabitants can vary from loose to tight, allowing for a range of spatial and social experience. A choreographically rich place can balance both clarity and memorability of place with the chance for serendipity and a multiplicity of experience in space and time.

From the Italian hill town to the Japanese fishing village, and on again to the north African town, it is most often in vernacular urbanism that we see the richest, most diverse types of expression of the fit between body movement and architecture. In the hill town, we move in close relationship to the poetry of the land form. In the fishing village, the branching out of streets from the water's edge into the foothills recapitulates the form of tributaries collecting water as they gradually move from the mountains down to the sea. The complexity of maze-like movement in the north African town seems both to reflect an inner-directed social structure and to celebrate a kinesthetic and topographic understanding of space— as distinct from more familiar Cartesian abstraction.

In Perugia, topography generates ramps, stairs, and bridges that choreograph our movements.

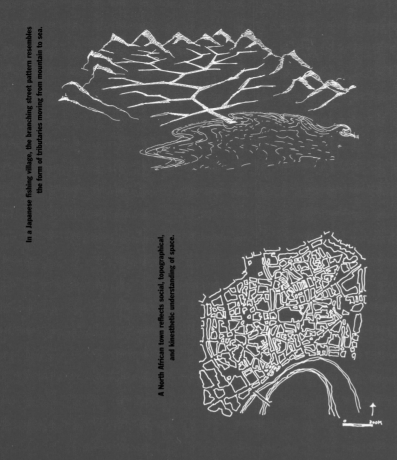

At the Crossroads School, we remodeled a warehouse into an art center and went beyond the "program" to organize the circulation spaces into powerful places of community. Three archetypal elements—a street, a plaza, and a stair are choreographed into a rich array of informal, dynamic, and flexible spaces. The internal street connects the city "address" of the campus with the informal life of its private alley. It is animated with studios, offices, and student lockers, each with identity along the passage. The plaza and stair provide places of social opportunity and focus.

LIGHT AND THE LAND

The changing states of light, climate, and vegetation can become active participants in creating dynamic architectural and social spaces. The properties of geology and topography, less mutable but imperceptibly shifting, can amplify specificity of place. With both static and temporal elements, places of community must relate to the environment of the place in its broadest sense.

Traditional Japanese architecture provides some of the most illuminating and subtle examples of poetic response to the natural environment. The traditional house weaves a subtle relationship between landscape, building, and inhabitant. While the body-based *tatami* module provides an underlying order, the shifting definitions of inside and out, framed views, and movable *shoji*s yield an architecture in which landscape, building, and inhabitant are harmonious in a mutually defined but varying type of unity.

At a much larger scale, we sought to design the new Walter A. Haas School of Business at UC Berkeley so that its 200,000 square feet of varied program would fit itself with sensitivity and richness into a tight and challenging site. Flanked by intimate residential scale, formal campus-scale buildings, and the dark natural beauty of Strawberry Creek, our plan evolved in close dialogue with the land and the light. The sinewy topographic movement of Strawberry Creek is extended into the major community space, which organizes business school life along a terraced landscaped street. Gateways to the school and views from it to the hills and bay are organized in relation to the movement of the land. In this cool climate, orientation to the southern light and warmth is carefully shaped for the important social gathering spaces. Building forms take cues from the hills beyond, and colors and materials forge careful connections to the surrounding landscape. The connection of building and environment enhances the specificity of this place and gives expression to the culture and community of the school.

CONCLUSION: SHAPING COMMUNITY

These five principles have been allies in our search to bring meaning to our buildings. The campus is a place where people of diverse backgrounds and attitudes come together for an intense period of study and communication, building a society that is at once transitory and lasting. The search for form and shape based on disciplined formal principles is congruent with the desire to shape places that fundamentally support and encourage the changing life of a community. With a sensitivity to light and land, scale, hierarchy, and geometry, we have sought in each venue to enhance community and express the unique potential of the institution and its place.

COMMUNITIES OF PURPOSE
by John Ruble

ESSAY

Campuses and their inhabitants constitute a distinct kind of community. With their special mix of permanent and transient populations and a broadly shared sense of purpose, these communities are defined and sustained by traditions, goals, and common experiences that profoundly inform the campus as a place. This is especially meaningful in the United States, where campuses have a staying power and a continuity of habitation and human investment rarely enjoyed by any other form of community. In all of our campus design work, the issues of continuity and change have been significant and complex. Our academic building projects often have become interventions to "restore" campus plans by reasserting the qualities of community and place that have eroded.

In designing our own long-range plans for two new campuses, one in Taiwan and one in Tacoma, Washington, our awareness has been sharpened by working elsewhere with such institutions as the University of California at Berkeley, California Institute of Technology, Pasadena, and the University of Oregon, where inspired initial plans have been adversely affected by the changing attitudes of higher education and its architects. How is it, one must ask, that well-loved campuses succeed in holding their identity despite the assault of time? What qualities make a campus recognizable after generations of boards, regents, planners, and architects have had a chance to redefine the mission of the institution several times over? While ideals and purposes change, how does a campus communicate its abiding sense of identity and continue to inspire appropriate responses by planners and architects?

We would like to propose a set of attributes that, in one combination or another, seem to us to be decisive in giving campuses a vital sense of community and purpose, and thereby to strengthen their chances for long-term survival.

FOUNDATION: SETTING APART

The act of "founding" is at the core of any institution, which must by definition be instituted in a particular place, at a particular time, to accomplish particular goals. This has always had special meaning on the American continent, where the campus as a place is central to the way we think of college and university. In much the same way as the original founding of the American colonies, the American college began with setting apart land and erecting buildings that both provided for and symbolized their purpose.

This act of establishment in time and in place became synonymous with the vital task of developing social order, as early colleges began to provide the lawyers, physicians, and teachers to build a civilization. Such high purposes were matched by great investment, and college buildings were initially the largest and most elaborate structures on the continent.*

*See Paul Venable Turner, *Campus.*

More important than the buildings themselves, or perhaps more lasting, is the piece of land that they help to define: if the Rotunda at the University of Virginia or Nassau Hall at Princeton holds a value, it is modest compared to The Lawn, or as it was first identified at Princeton, The Campus. One cannot, of course, imagine these places in isolation from the buildings around them, but the setting apart of the "green" that will never be built upon is an eloquent statement of transcendent purpose.

Our campus plans at Tacoma and Dong-Hwa therefore began with a "clearing," which was rather simple on the Taiwan site, consisting almost entirely of sugar cane fields framed by mountains and rivers. In Tacoma, where a new campus has been planned within an existing city grid of streets and buildings, it was no less urgent to establish a series of "founding-places" by successively claiming and redefining the streetscape. Our plan calls for a set of squares stepping up the hill along 19th Street, culminating in a large, green commons with a striking view of Mount Rainier. These secured open spaces provide each campus with a legacy of connectedness to its geographic region.

FORM AND HIERARCHY

The campuses we admire most often involve a spatial diagram or composition. Whether clear and instantly memorable like Jefferson's Academical Village, or full of subtle twists like Cope and Stewardson's plan for Washington University in St. Louis, the establishment of a formal order builds on the initial meanings of the founding green and elaborates the idea of order into a set of relationships between the parts.

Jefferson's diagram, for example, grew from a domestic, frontier model of education: groups of students gathered around a hearth in the teacher's home, learning in a kind of Socratic exchange. In turn, ranges of student rooms embrace the temple-houses of learning gathered

Jefferson's university:
Campus as a diagram of academic order.

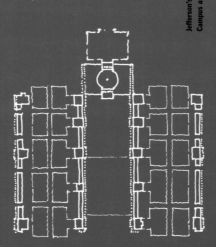

around the lawn and the library: an elegant hierarchy from individual, to group, to collective place.

Jefferson's splendid composition seems rather static compared to Washington University, where the rewards of movement and exploration are a principal theme. Entering simply enough through a central gate to an enclosed quad, one is soon drawn through a field of shifting axes and dynamic balances to a larger, more loosely defined green, where a large, off-center chapel hall fires an allée like a cannon shot into the landscape beyond.

However compelling they are, such diagrams seldom rule for long; all colleges and universities outgrow their initial plans, and over the life of the institution, the idea of order is subject to constant revision. Ideally, this process can

Dong-Hwa University:
Graded field and meandering water.

become a kind of grand collaboration across decades, as at Princeton, where generations of architects and educators slowly built up richly varied sequences around Nassau Hall and its original open fields.

Our own plans for Dong-Hwa and Tacoma are examples of formal order coming to terms with site conditions in a play of order and incident. At Dong-Hwa, the founding field lies at the formal center, around which academic courtyard buildings are set into a grid of broad, tree-shaded boulevards. This formal inner precinct is separated from adjacent residential villages by a meandering water-park that cuts into the grid unexpectedly. Students bicycle across bridges to enter the academic center, a movement between divided worlds inspired by traditional Chinese gardens and temple complexes.

Bridges animate Dong-Hwa's grid of boulevards.

In Tacoma, an academic order is worked into an existing city plan by carving out central places in the street grid and heightening existing axes and vistas. The rich pattern of geometric lines already found on-site has been elaborated into a large figure-ground of buildings and open space. At key points in the plan, existing and proposed landmark buildings provide destinations and frame passages for the movement of students up and down the hill. This movement uses the streets, which are at intervals transformed into walks and stairs.

A third and unbuilt plan we developed for Kao-Shiung Institute of Technology, also in Taiwan, proposes an altogether different order. As a national highway divided the site, it was first necessary to link the two halves, which we proposed to do with a grand boulevard. This main street would provide a rich sequence of places, along which the highway crossing was simply one more event. Metaphorically inspired by splendid Chinese scroll paintings depicting mythical journeys, the street is a procession of daily student life from residence to class, from library (meditative state) to sport fields (active state), punctuated by urban squares, formal gardens, and criss-crossing geometries.

Kao Shiung University: Campus as narrative journey.

From Emperor Kwangsi's Southern journey; Early Chinese distinction of "Town and Gown."

PLACEMENT AND IDENTITY

An important advantage of a spatial diagram is that individual buildings within the scheme can enjoy special identity, a pride of place that is not dependent on their size and use. One of the most dramatic examples of this power of positioning is at the Greenwich Royal Hospital, where Christopher Wren's Baroque domes and colonnades are subservient to Inigo Jones' earlier, delicately scaled Queen's House, which Wren was asked to retain in the center of his grand plan.

We sought this kind of sovereignty for the existing Snoqualmie Falls Power Substation in the Tacoma plan to give greater eminence to its important new function as the campus library. The building's rotation off the typical street grid is picked up in a new axis, allowing this historic building to preside over spaces yet to be realized in the campus plan. In the Dong-Hwa plan, the library is also placed at the center of the campus world, as part of an axis that includes a large "villa" for central administration and the student union's complex of auditoria and dining halls. The public purposes of these shared facilities, analogous to civic buildings in an urban grid, are heightened by their relation to the plan.

As campuses have traditionally had problems with certain building types that typically end up dominating the view from across town (research laboratories, stadia, and sprawling medical centers, for example), it becomes critical to establish formal orders capable of including them. At Dong-Hwa, the main axis ends in the athletics field house, helping to draw the gargantuan sports complex into the composition.

RHETORICAL FABRIC

The architectural style of campus development has always served to define purpose: Gothic to spur on the revival of collegiate affiliation, Georgian to remind us of the critical role of founding principles in the birth of a culture, and more recently Modernism, to establish once and for all the freedom of the institution to evolve according to its needs. Once these causes have faded in time, what seems important about style is that it becomes identified with the character of the campus as a place. For any new design that seeks to uphold the campus ethos, style has particular relevance.

Scale seems to be critical to the uses of style. Small campuses like Cal Tech in Pasadena, or the Claremont Colleges, work well with a singular idiom, which it seems urgent not to contradict. Large, complex campuses like the University of Washington benefit from variation, but only so much. The ravaged Berkeley campus of the 1960s and '70s shows the limits to which the fabric of a powerful core can be contradicted by alternative forms. In our own work at Berkeley, we sought to support the existence of major and minor themes—the major being the Italianate/City Beautiful, which is complemented wonderfully by the minor Bay Area Shingle-style of the faculty clubs. Our Haas School of Business and William Turnbull's Foothill Housing complex both seek to extend this minor theme, adding to the campus a set of finely grained buildings and places that move in close connection with the natural landscape.

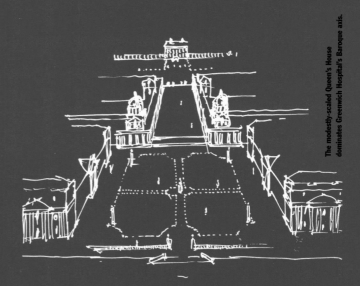

The modestly-scaled Queen's House dominates Greenwich Hospital's Baroque axis.

THE PLACE OF RITUAL

Academic communities, more than any others, are enriched by colorful traditions of habitation. The wild goings-on in Auerbach's Keller, where Faust and his student friends drained kegs of wine the size of Winnebagos, are the same activities which inspired so many college founders to seek sites remote from any town. Fortunately, towns inevitably grew up around such campuses, and lively student traditions evolved within.

One tends to forget that 17th-century colleges such as Harvard and William and Mary did not start out with football teams or fraternities. These and other institutions took root and came to enrich academic community life, along with student activist groups and ethnic studies programs, during some 200 years of development.

Both formally sanctioned rituals like commencement processions and less formal events such as Princeton's "P-rade" require places of enactment: streets, parade grounds, and grand halls that enrich the repertoire of campus places and connect past and present traditions. Some of these extracurricular traditions have radical formal contributions to make: the football stadium, for example, is usually the largest structure ever built on a campus and provides the grandest community rituals in rhythm with the changing seasons.

University of Virginia:
The "graffiti" of secret societies.

Equally important are smaller campus societies that make their presence known in other ways, such as the windowless buildings of Yale's secret societies. My favorite is the elegant graffiti with which secret organizations such as the "Z" Society and "IMP" mark the venerable stairs and walls at the University of Virginia. The fact that someone has to keep replacing the painted signs speaks mysteriously and eloquently of a living tradition.

Perhaps of all of our built campus works to date, the Haas Business School at Berkeley most invites this kind of evolving tradition, and we are confident that future generations will not fail to take notice: there are arches from which banners may unfurl, perches from which to speak, grand stairs and gardens calling for processions, bronze bears to be dressed up, and a vast, unfinished attic waiting to be explored.

REAL ACCIDENTS

Interview with John Ruble and Buzz Yudell

INTERVIEW

This interview was conducted on April 20, 1995, by James Mary O'Connor, Mark Denton, Stephen Harby, and Wendy Kohn.

QUESTION You have compared Moore Ruble Yudell's design process to jazz improvisation. How does this work?

BUZZ YUDELL Well, if you look at a wonderful jazz group, it tends to be four or five very talented musicians who may have slightly different ways of seeing things but also tend to agree on certain things. It's not a paradigm of collectivism versus a single artist hero. It's a group of artists working together. It's what we agree on that allows the differences to come into play.

Q In other words, you don't have someone sitting at a piano just randomly playing the keys.

BY I think we have a fairly broad set of shared values about the humanistic principles of architecture. You could talk about a number of underlying beliefs that I think are shared throughout the office—about connecting to place, connecting to people, about architecture that is connected to tradition but also explores contemporary art and culture... yet always coming back to how buildings are places and are inhabited at various scales.

 **JOHN RUBLE** That's true, although I think that a lot of the things we do on the very specific level of design come from what Charles Moore described as enthusiasms, or things that you personally respond to. We have a lot in common here as well, in terms of places we've seen that we like.... The enthusiasms that influence what we do on one project or another come out of experiencing places we all admire.

Q So there's a context within which the exploration occurs—a sense of harmony—of what has value.

BY At the core, one thing that is very strong is a conviction or optimism that architecture can actually counter some of the contemporary disorientation we see and can stand for values that are fundamental—a sense of shared habitation, or shared separation even, as opposed to architecture that embodies a chaotic, hopeless, contemporary society.

Q There are architects who find that the only appropriate response to the current context is to rebel...or to reflect chaos.

B Y One thing that's really unfortunate is that the ideas that people like Charles Moore and Robert Venturi were expressing 30 years ago, about fundamental traditions of inhabiting places—quite rebellious at the time—were taken by some people to be just about historicism. What they're really about is basic human needs and aspirations and desires. Just because the Machine Age followed the Agrarian Age and is followed by the Information Age and chaos theory doesn't mean that we don't biologically and emotionally and spiritually still have very fundamental needs that architecture can satisfy. I think we're at our best when we're expressing not just a superficial image of a place, but really connecting to its deeper spirit and history.

Q And does this relate to style?

B Y The debate now is not necessarily between Modernism and something that is historically connected. I think it's more of a discussion about architecture that is still based on humanism, versus architecture that is based on something else, whether it's the analogy of the machine or the analogy of abstract linguistic theory. I think you can find lots of "Modern" architecture, like a lot of Tadao Ando's work, that is very beautifully connected to place, where there's a sense of inhabitation and procession. It's unfortunate the media has ended up making this kind of modernism versus Post-Modernism argument. You can cut through and find historicist work that doesn't make wonderful places and very modern work that does.

J R Our interest in history, in valued places, is both emotional and analytic. I guess for us the creation of a place, whether it's light coming through the window, or movement across a landscape, is the experience. You don't need to create an analogy to that. The order should inform the experience, rather than substitute for it.

B Y There's a sort of discipline related to geometry as one aspect, or abstraction related to the land as another aspect. I think something that we do very well is to discover how form roots itself to the experience of the land and the landscape.

Q And where does history enter the work?

B Y We're free to draw on history as a sort of continuum. Here we are in 1996, we're part of that continuum, and we can equally look for inspiration in the year 20 B.C., or the

year 1450, 1920, or 1996. There's not necessarily a predetermined positive or negative about any one of those periods. But I think the vernacular is a big influence in the sense that there are a lot of principles in vernacular architecture that are essentially what we're talking about. It's about how people make places that they understand in relation to places they know, and their culture, and themselves. So when you look at hill towns, for example, or places in Mexico—places made over time by many people—there's an incredible wonder and richness in terms of architecture.

J R There's also a kind of pragmatic simplicity about vernacular architecture that I think becomes more and more influential for us.

B Y One thing we're not is ideological.

> "It's about how people make places that they understand in relation to places they know."

141

Q And yet while it seems clear that Moore Ruble Yudell's work isn't meant to be distressing or profoundly alienating— the idea is not simply to make work that reinforces everybody's expectations or preconceptions. Can you both talk about that?

B Y Originality comes from a process of exploring, that within the design process there's a dynamic of conversation and critiquing built-in—it's almost as if we're sketching when we're talking, or talking when we're sketching. It's a kind of conversation that builds on itself and creates a broader image of greater depth.

J R   And as Buzz said earlier, we're not trying to reach a point where we're all trying to do one thing. We don't believe there is *one* way to respond to any problem. But we are doing things in an interactive way. Someone sketches an idea, and that goes to someone else who has his or her take on it, and maybe does something unexpected with it. It becomes an interesting process.

B Y   As an aside, I think it's interesting that all architects collaborate...it's just that a lot of them don't think they do.

J R   Within collaboration, the overall direction comes from an evolving sense of appropriateness. Each project develops a kind of a story or a set of themes, and that begins to tell you what to do next.

J R   One of the things that we feel good about, in terms of our built work, is that people value it. Part of the optimism, or the positive, affirmative part, is that we find people have values invested in the architecture that will last. People who have been involved in the design process value the building—it means a lot to them. One indicator of this is that they take care of the buildings. So we're working, I think, very much towards finding those kinds of fundamental values that people can bring to architecture and which will live long past the design and construction process.

"Each project develops a
kind of a story or a set
of themes..."

Q   For the past 15 years or so, you have used a technique of client workshops, in which you design a variety of exercises to help institutional clients communicate their aspirations for a building. You've both talked about these work sessions as one way of discovering certain kinds of values and connections. How does this collaboration with the client contribute to the architecture?

J R   That's a good point to make...about the workshops: they extend collaboration as a process—which means individuals can take part, but it also becomes a way of exploring place. The workshops are about helping us discover what values are invested in places by people who are there or who belong there—whether it's a campus, or a town, or a house. Then it's not just our reactions as visitors or as architects that go into the design. I  think the collaboration in the workshop sense is a way of getting a lot more depth to what is valued in a place, and therefore becomes a design instrument.

B Y   This relates to another theme about collaboration, which is that underlying the ability to collaborate is a sense that one can learn. One doesn't know everything about a place, whether it's Oregon, or Berlin, or Taiwan. Or even amongst ourselves, critiquing or bouncing ideas off each other, we enjoy hearing each other's partially formulated ideas...creativity isn't a finite entity, and doesn't have to be a one-man show.

Q   Do you think this interchange—which is clearly so much a part of the design process—gets expressed in the buildings?

J R   There is a kind of community spirit, almost like something that allows you to participate, as opposed to a building that just exists on its own, reflecting on its own perfect order, which doesn't need anything else.

B Y   One thing that seems to happen quite often is that we find an interstitial space or places of connection in a plan, and see them as sort of living, rich places, sometimes with uses we hadn't thought of. Oftentimes, this is how we shape spaces between buildings, or the spaces beside buildings. It's a way of taking what would have been circulation space and collecting it in such a way that it becomes a place of community.

JR   This is reminding me of something I remember encountering when I was in the Peace Corps in Tunisia...which is that we thought a lot about why the Tunisians, whenever they would greet each other or sit down to do some business, would spend so much time just chatting and having tea and doing all these other things. Someone explained that the fact of two people sitting down together to talk to each other and have a meeting was more important than any particular subject they might have to talk about. And so you don't just jump into the business at hand. You exchange respect and celebrate the fact that here is one person and another person sitting down to meet each other and to spend time together. This is one of the most important things that buildings can do. They can remind us that we're gathering together, and that's actually as important as anything we might do afterwards.

BY   Community itself is the ultimate function.

Q   In certain projects you have been asked to create the entire place yourself, in some of the master plans for entire campuses, for example. What have become the generating ideas for these projects?

JR   I think of a campus as a place where in a very abstract or general way, order and hierarchy are important. There should be a center. There should be a place where the whole thing started, on which everything else builds.

"Underlying the ability to collaborate is a sense that one can learn."

Q You root the community in a particular place.

J R Yes, and in the process we're not inclined to ride roughshod over lots of little traces that are on the site. When we first came to places like Karow, Germany, or Dong-Hwa, Taiwan, there were some very specific things in the site, and there was also a kind of blankness because we were planning on what were basically big, wide-open fields. We had to look extra hard and had to be very quiet and listen to qualities that weren't necessarily shouting at us the way they might, say, on the University of Maryland campus. I think it's a process of refining latent forms and making them stronger. And I guess the fewer things there are, the more a certain feature of the site becomes an important theme, because it's available. At Dong-Hwa it was just the fact that there was a river near the site. This confrontation of the formal with a kind of craggy landscape suited us very well because we've always liked the idea of order and accident somehow interweaving and affecting each other.

B Y One of the main themes of our work is basically a dialectic: there's a tension between different kinds of order on the one hand, and the events of chance and circumstance on the other. The fundamental and the circumstantial, if you will. And we think that's not just an arbitrary dichotomy, because each of those is a potent and meaningful aspect of life. Fundamentals are kind of timeless and beautiful things that people connect to, and the circumstantial things are not just arbitrary but relate to a particular place in time and space. In that sense the opportunity for making a synthesis out of this dialectic comes from two

"Given a choice between real accidents
and pretend accidents, we'd rather work
with the real accidents."

very different parts of the universe—order and accident—that we believe are both part of the whole. Both essential, and both a part of everyday life.

J R That's why the original site as a place is so important to us: given a choice between real accidents and pretend accidents, we'd rather work with the real accidents.

IN PROGRESS

The Hugh and Hazel Darling library addition at the UCLA
School of Law sets ambitious goals for both context and use.
The site is a busy corner at an important campus gateway,
adjoining the existing law school complex. A new tower marks
this corner along a major campus axis, responding to neighboring
historic buildings such as the tower of Dodd Hall. Its materials
and composition offer a fresh interpretation of UCLA's traditional
scale, massing, and materials, including patterned brick, pre-cast
concrete trim, and glass.

To the north of this new tower, the facade of the addition follows the
gentle curve of Circle Drive, taking full advantage of the restricted
site. To the south, arcaded terraces accessible from fourth-floor
faculty offices overlook a new south-facing entry courtyard that
incorporates access ramps and tranquil seating. The renovation
also provides separate, direct access to the library for late-hour use.

The interior of the project emphasizes clarity of organization as
well as continuity and contiguity of the collection. A dramatic
stair connecting all levels provides vertical continuity and a central
point of orientation for readers. The renovated main reading

HUGH AND HAZEL DARLING LAW LIBRARY ADDITION

University of California, Los Angeles, California

room and other public reading areas are located on the main
floor adjacent to the collection, while more secluded reading
rooms on upper floors provide spaces primarily for the use of
the UCLA law community. Reading areas in the southeast corner
tower offer especially dramatic views and natural light. New
faculty offices are located adjacent to existing offices on the
second, third, and fourth floors, offering convenient communication among new and existing facilities. Materials and
finishes, including wood ceilings, wainscoting, and shelving,
reinforce continuity with the law school's best existing spaces.

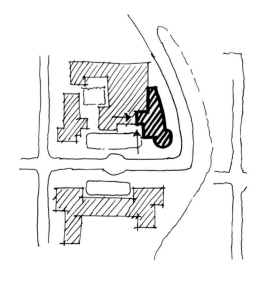

The addition to the Law Library provides a gateway to the greater
campus and helps to establish clear new entry points.

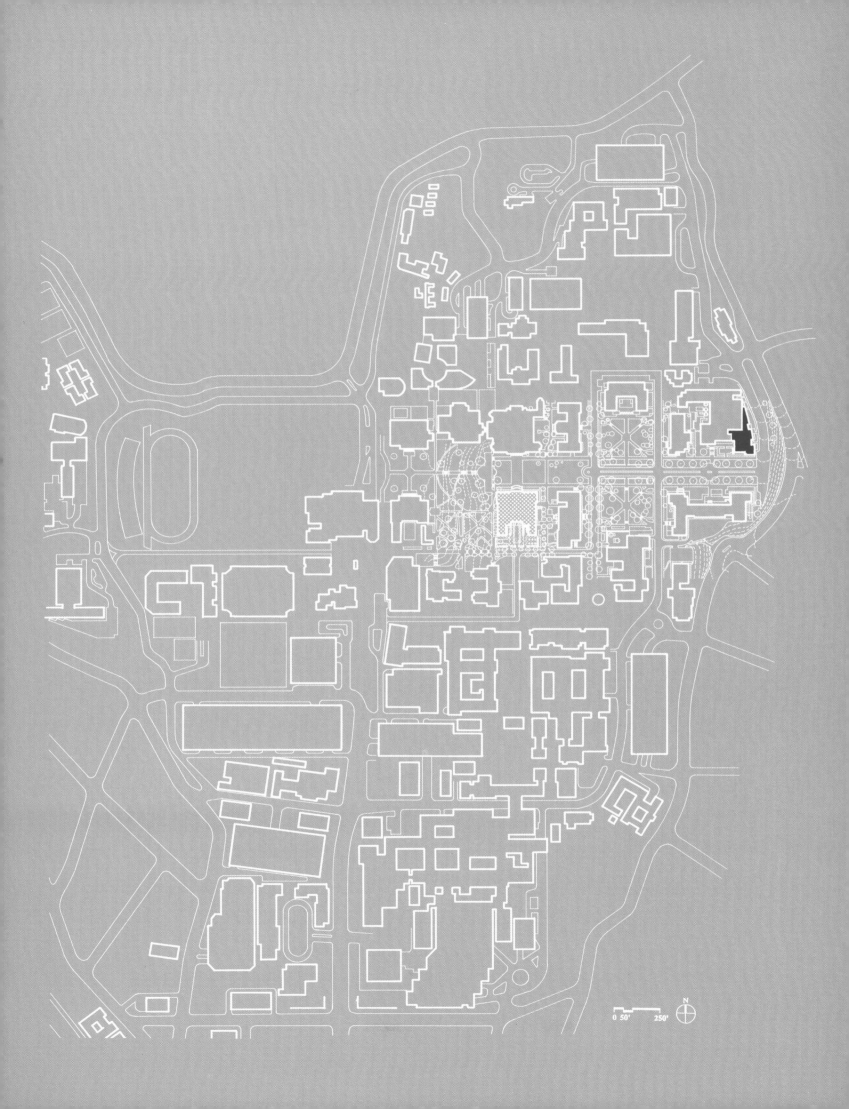

0 50'   250'   N

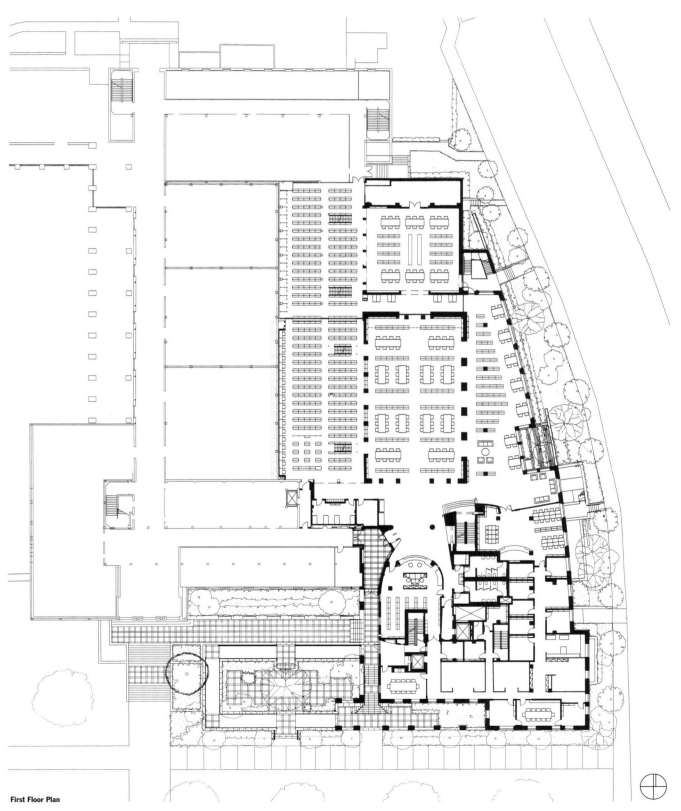

First Floor Plan

The massing of the addition culminates in a corner tower.

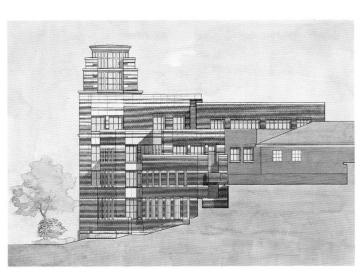

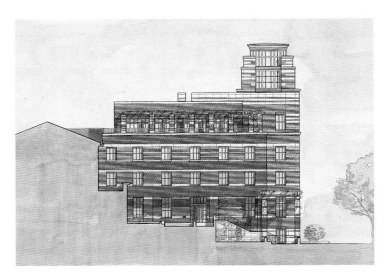

149

The building infills former street setbacks to create its site.

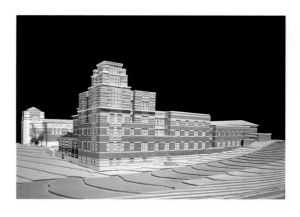

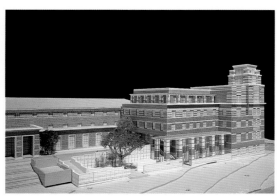

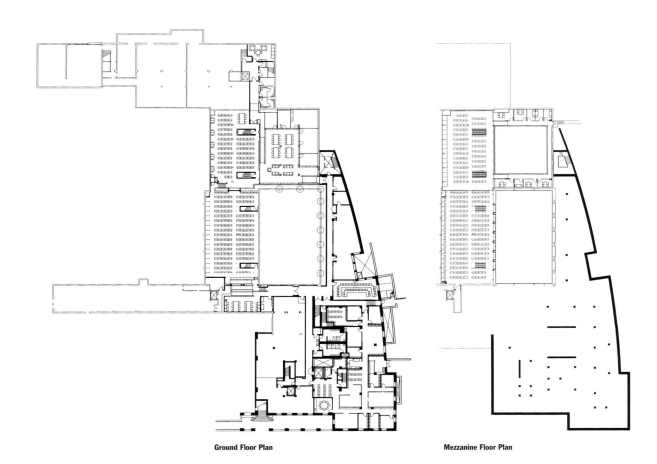

Ground Floor Plan

Mezzanine Floor Plan

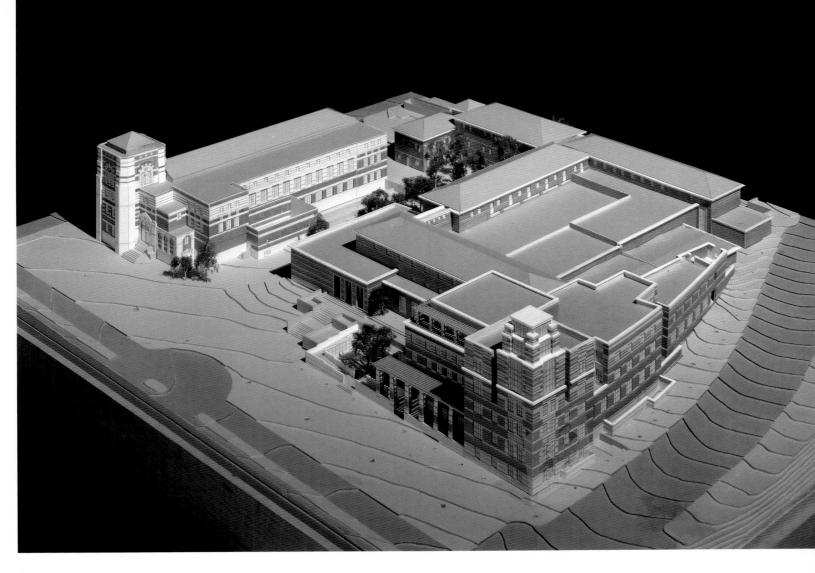

The new tower sets up a dialogue with the existing tower of neighboring Dodd Hall.

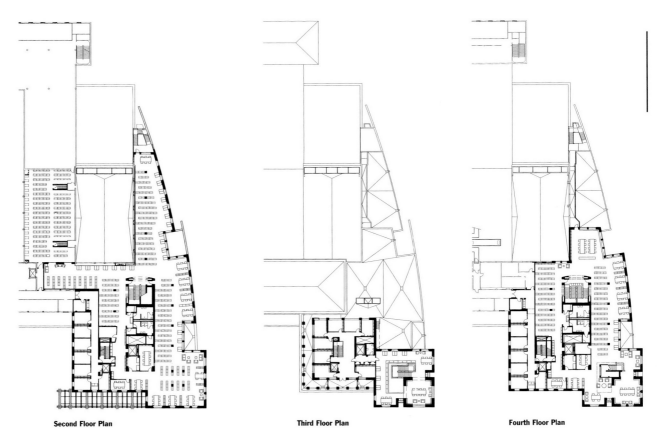

Second Floor Plan   Third Floor Plan   Fourth Floor Plan

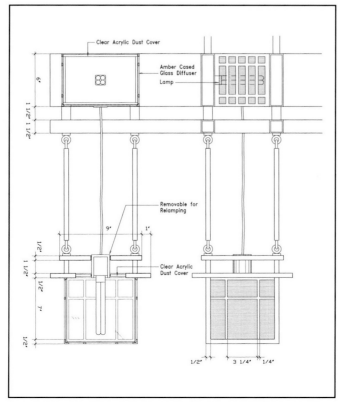

Clear Acrylic Dust Cover

Amber Cased
Glass Diffuser

Lamp

Removable for
Relamping

Clear Acrylic
Dust Cover

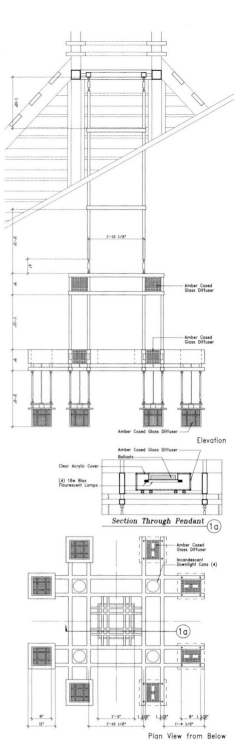

Amber Cased
Glass Diffuser

Amber Cased
Glass Diffuser

Amber Cased Glass Diffuser

Elevation

Amber Cased Glass Diffuser

Ballasts

Clear Acrylic Cover

(4) 18w Biax
Flourescent Lamps

Section Through Pendant 1a

Amber Cased
Glass Diffuser

Incandescent
Downlight Cans (4)

1a

Plan View from Below

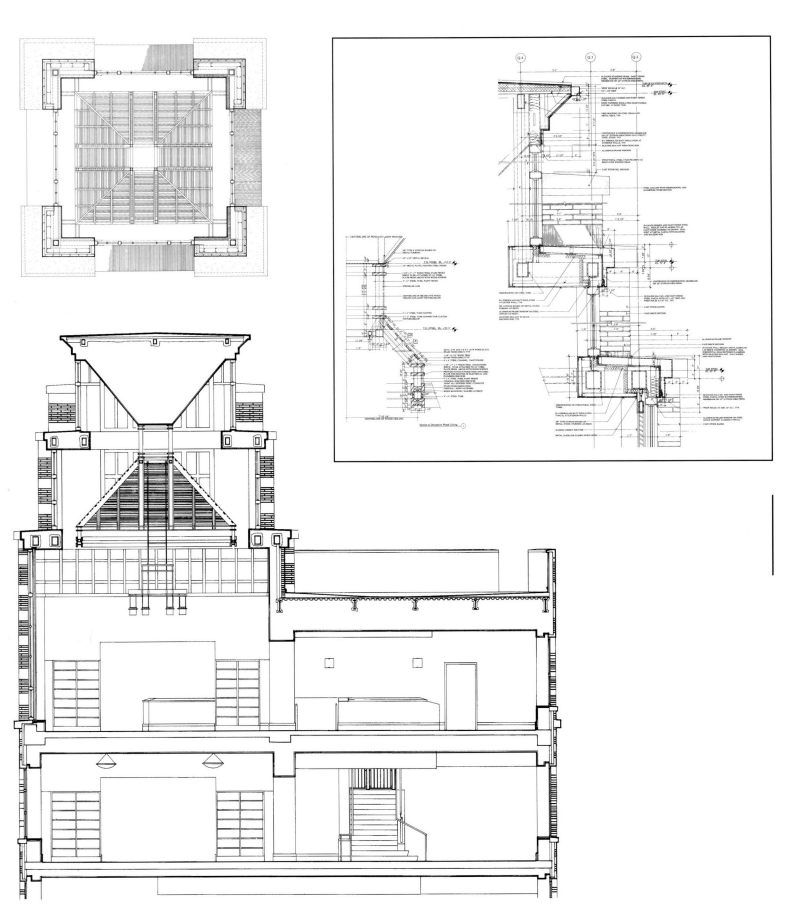

155

Avery House provides living accommodations for 140 under-graduates and graduate students, and it includes five faculty apartments as well. An important goal of the project is to increase interaction among students and faculty outside the classroom and laboratory and offer comfortable settings for a wide variety of activities and events: from meals and casual discussion to lectures, performances, and celebrations. Moore Ruble Yudell's approach has been to create a hierarchical layering of architectural and planning responses, encouraging multiple readings and uses of the places created.

Avery House is organized around four interconnected court-yards, each with a distinctive character. The largest, "Commons Court," is the arrival point for the complex, accessible through an arcade from a major pedestrian campus mall. The dining hall, cafe, lounges, conference rooms, and library face Commons Court, and arcades and porches surround a raised dining terrace and shaded main courtyard. Beyond a gated entrance to the secure residential section of Avery House, a broad courtyard opens, perfect for Frisbee or volleyball. Two smaller courts, one a shaded grove of Chinese flame trees, the

AVERY HOUSE, CALIFORNIA INSTITUTE OF TECHNOLOGY

Pasadena, California

other dominated by a human-scale chessboard, are raised slightly from the larger court to distinguish their boundaries without losing visual and spatial continuity.

Inside, entryways featuring social stairs are placed to encour-age interaction near lounges, showers, and laundry rooms. Student lounges are placed in the project's two towers, where they enjoy prominent locations and commanding views.

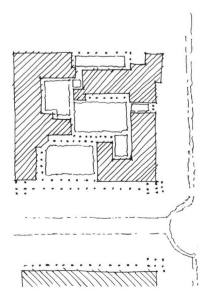

Simple building elements give shape to the hierarchy of courtyards.

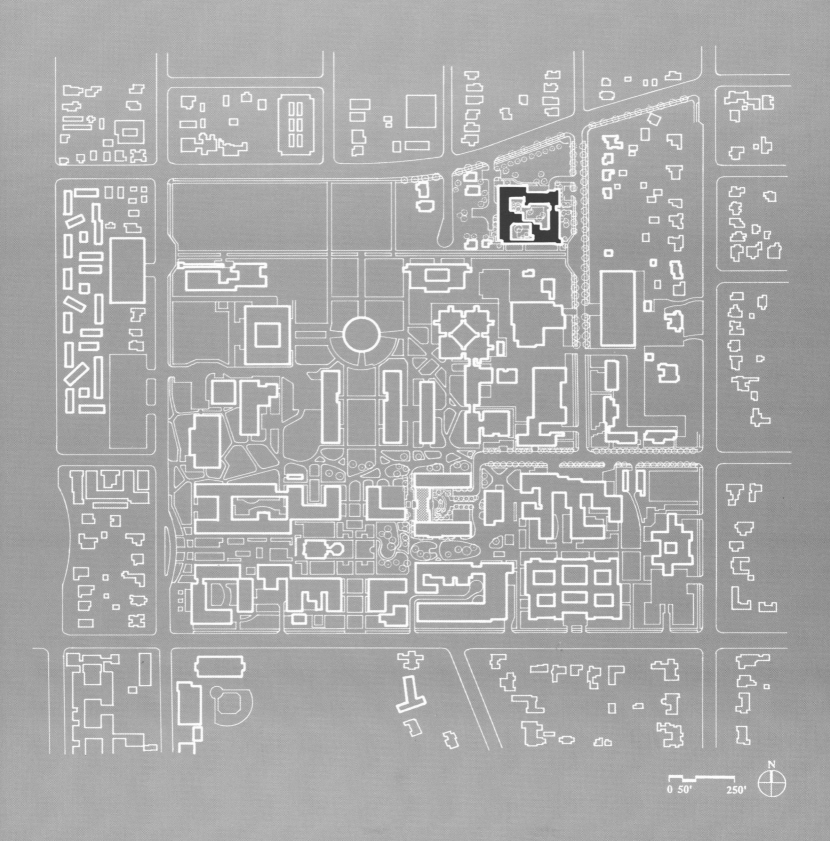

0 50'　250'

N

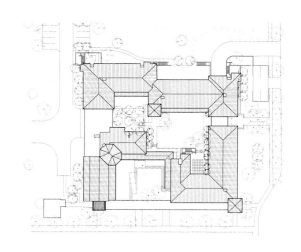

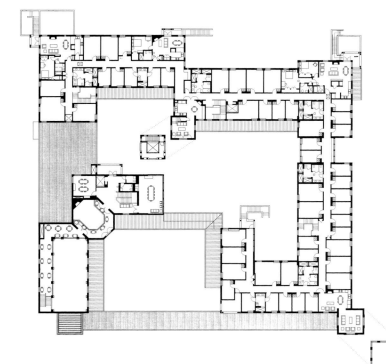

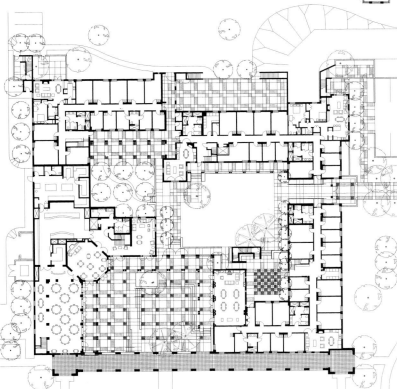

Public rooms surround Commons Court; student and faculty rooms form interlocking residential courtyards.

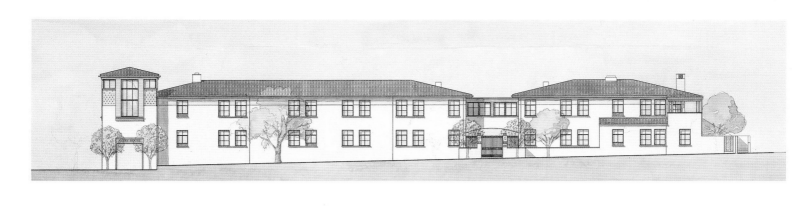

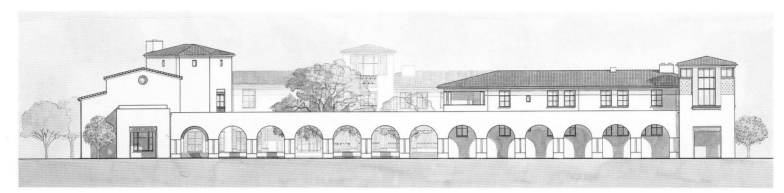

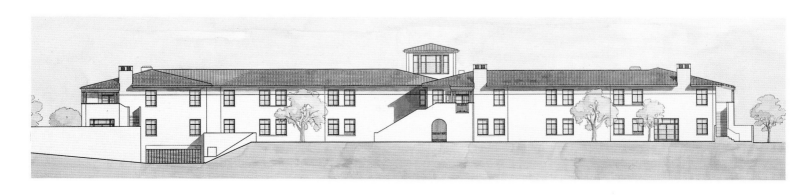

The approach from campus through an arcade leads to Commons Court.

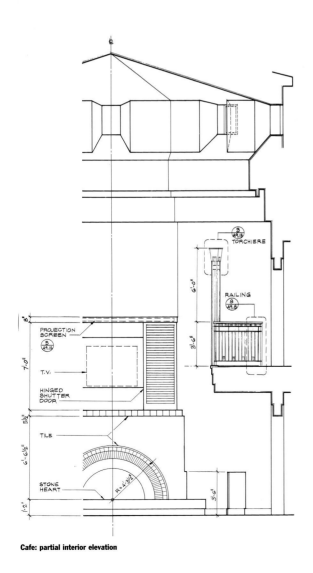

Cafe: partial interior elevation

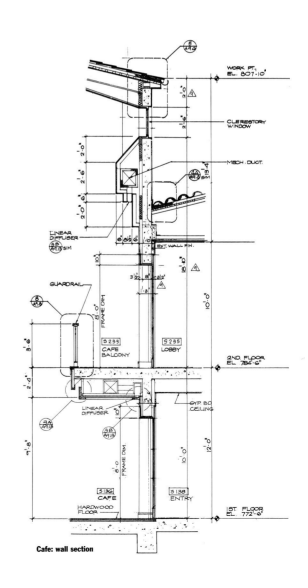

Cafe: wall section

The hierarchical layering of spaces continues from the overall form of the project into public rooms such as the dining hall.

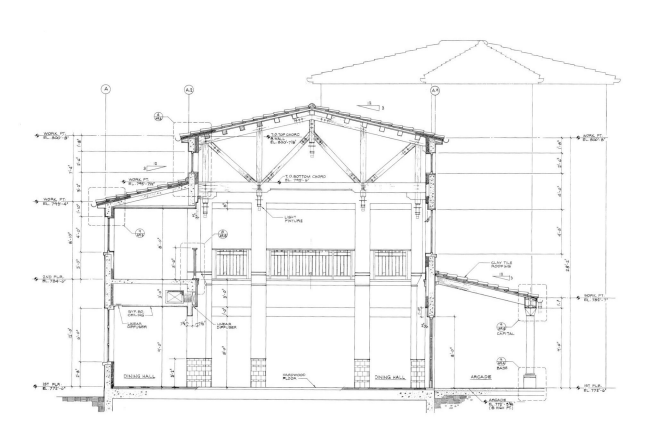

Moore Ruble Yudell's design for the Maryland Center for the Performing Arts enhances the fabric of campus life as it celebrates the broad range of performing arts in a regional facility. As an integrated part of the West Campus master plan, the Center is conceived as a coherent whole that responds to extremely varied adjacent site conditions. Configured as an "academic village," it is organized around open spaces and courtyards shaped to establish points of entry, enhance views, and provide a variety of social and activity spaces. The massing of the project reflects the primary design intent. Performance halls, departmental entries, lounges, and the library are given strong readings within the whole, while support areas are expressed more quietly. The scale of the larger building elements is modulated by elements of intermediate height and low arcades, creating comfortably-scaled open spaces.

The major entry plaza for the Maryland Center for Performing Arts welcomes vehicles and pedestrians with entries to the library, music, theater, and dance departments. A grand processional sequence moves from this entry plaza, anchored by a marquee tower, through a clerestory-lit lobby

MARYLAND CENTER FOR PERFORMING ARTS, UNIVERSITY OF MARYLAND

College Park, Maryland

that serves as a piazza for all major performance halls. It continues on to the restaurant and out to a dining court and landscaped amphitheater beyond. Along this grand and celebratory sequence each major hall has a strong identity with its own portico. Balconies from each hall overlook the lobby, providing ample opportunity to see and be seen. Strong colors are layered to add richness and drama to the space. Structured parking wraps the football stadium to the south with a new facade, directly connected to the Center and serving the West Campus of the university as well.

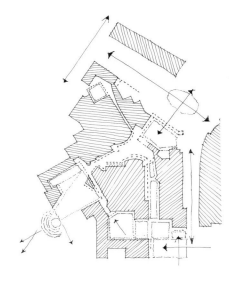

The building resolves the geometries of adjacent districts while creating departmental courtyards and the major lobby "street."

Reflections on the Project by Roger Lewis

Professor, School of Architecture, University of Maryland; architecture critic for *The Washington Post*

and Stephen Hurtt

Dean, School of Architecture, University of Maryland

The University of Maryland at College Park is a campus struggling to define and project its image. Originally a land-grant agricultural college, it has recently matured into a selective and comprehensive research university. The campus core consists of neo-Georgian Colonial Revival buildings of some merit, along with an array of larger, more recent buildings with unconvincing Classical and Georgian veneers. These nevertheless provide visual cohesiveness to the university.

The performance halls of the Maryland Center for Performing Arts are shaped to encourage a close relationship between every member of the audience and the performers. They are placed to enhance lively communication on an intimate scale. Each space has the potential for "tuning" or variable acoustics, with its basic geometry set to the most demanding acoustical response required. The Concert Hall, built high and relatively narrow with massive materials, surrounds a capacity audience with the sound produced by an orchestra and chorus. When smaller groups perform, interrelated systems of adjustable absorption elements adjust the acoustical response of the room for optimal conditions. In the recital hall, similar variable acoustics systems provide support for musicians and tailor the listening experience for the audience. In the proscenium theater, the fixed acoustical environment is oriented toward opera and ballet.

The core campus is surrounded by seas of asphalt parking lots, a total of 19,000 spaces. Despite its size, this commuter campus is running out of building room as it undergoes a transition to a pattern of parking garages linked with a more sensible road network. All of this means that parking, athletic facilities, new academic structures, and an expanding adult-education and conference center all have competed for a place in the west campus area where the Maryland Center for Performing Arts (MCPA) is to be situated, threatening the remnants of a beautiful, rolling landscape. And while the university recently completed a pragmatic—but minimally visionary—campus plan, there exists no codified planning process.

To understand the design problem that Moore Ruble Yudell confronted, and to understand the responsiveness and quality of Moore Ruble Yudell's competition-winning project, one must understand something of the history of the university and its form. The original campus was a U-shaped cluster of buildings, a quadrangle on a hilltop facing east toward the old Post Road connecting Washington, D.C. and Baltimore. This original quad established the orthogonal pattern for the future campus and its primary east-west axial orientation. Important as it was, the original quad is scarcely perceptible today, eclipsed by the primary axial space of the campus, McKeldin Mall.

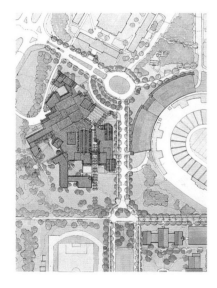

Planned in the 1920s and 1930s, the mall remains one of the largest in the United States. Just to the north of the original quad, stretching east-west, McKeldin Mall lies in a shallow valley such that the comparatively small buildings defining its spatial edges are given added importance by their elevation above the lawn. Trailing off to the south-east and past the original quad, groups of low-rise dormitories step down a gentle hillside to the town of College Park. North of McKeldin Mall, major expansion between the 1950s and 1980s produced buildings much larger than those of the earlier campus, but not conforming to a spatial ordering pattern on the scale of the mall. Rather, they simply face Campus Drive, a road parallel to the mall along the ridge forming the primary topographic feature enclosing the mall's north side. North of this ridge is another valley, the site of athletic fields and amphitheater-like football and baseball stadiums. Still farther north, and dominating the next ridge, stands a cluster of identical high-rise slab dormitories. To the west is a comparatively open site dominated by parking lots and large enough to accommodate the entire main campus of Columbia, Rice, or Princeton. The 1990 campus master plan called for westward extension of the mall axis across this site to link the center of campus with the Center for Adult Education. The remainder of the site was reserved for athletic fields.

On the surface, the design issues presented by the MCPA might seem simple enough. Below the surface, however, lies an extremely complex reality. The project's scope was daunting: respond to a two-inch-thick program document years in preparation by the university; develop a plan for a major sector of the campus yet to be occupied; within that projected campus sector plan, design the performing arts center complex on a preselected site; and, most important, create a landmark building related to the existing campus plan and architecture.

Housing the departments of music, theater, and dance, the 300,000-square-foot, $100 million project includes five separate public performance spaces—a 1,200-seat dedicated concert hall, a 350-seat recital hall, a 650-seat proscenium theater for drama and opera, a 200-seat experimental theater, and a 200-seat dance studio. Surrounding these are a performing-arts library, classrooms, faculty offices, rehearsal spaces, complete back-of-the-house support facilities, and a restaurant.

The Center for Performing Arts is sited on a set of existing athletic fields located on the edge of campus. The selection of this site was contrary to land uses projected by the campus master plan. But open exploration of alternative sites within this campus precinct was precluded by the desire for significant presence on University Boulevard, the press of the schedule, and commitments of other land parcels to other projects. It was clear from the start that a plan for the west campus, coupled with construction of the Maryland Center for Performing Arts, would establish the armature for the future growth of the west campus well into the next century.

Moore Ruble Yudell analyzed existing spatial patterns of the campus and recognized several primary organizational characteristics: the orthogonal geometry related to the mall; the diagonal of the ridge; the composition of many smaller spaces—quadrangles and courtyards—running from the south dormitories across the site of the original campus through Tawes Plaza; a major pathway of student movement extending across the parking garage site to the MCPA; and the campus' formal and informal, or Classical and Romantic, landscape traditions.

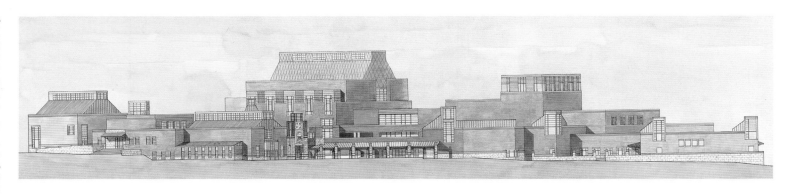

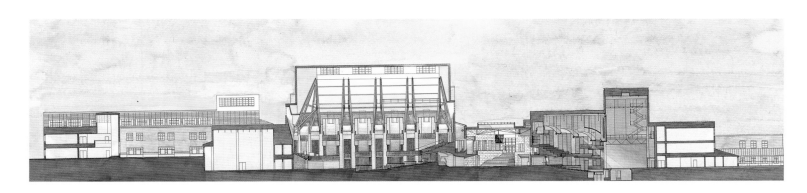

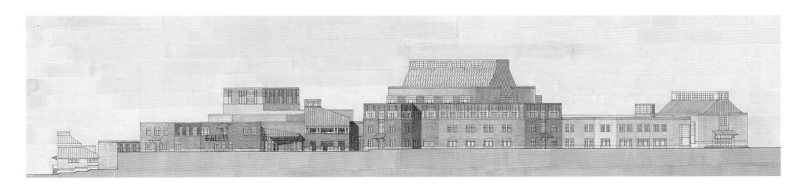

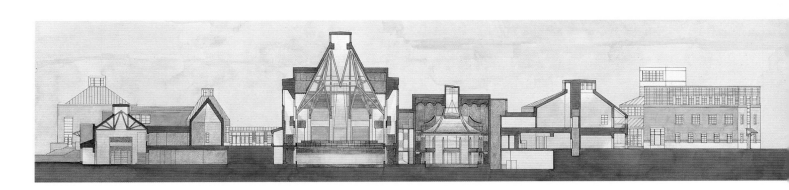

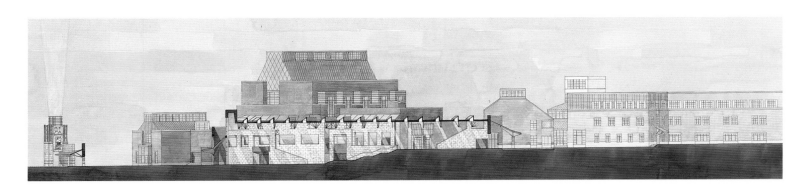

The proposed MCPA and west campus site plan radically transforms the university's master plan. University Boulevard, a divided, four-lane parkway, is an important regional artery, but has been the back door to campus. On this site, the MCPA displaces athletic fields and requires that this back door be transformed into a new front door, a significant campus gateway to numerous and diverse public activities—music, theater, dance, and opera performances as well as football, basketball, baseball, soccer, rugby, lacrosse, track, and tennis—and it requires the provision of parking areas to serve almost the entire campus.

Essential to Moore Ruble Yudell's master plan is a primary north-south axis and circulation spine, traversing the west campus and constituting a new "street" in the best sense of the word. Along this street would be a series of important entrances and spaces: the oval at campus drive; the plaza in front of Tawes; the splitting of the road to define a new quadrangular space that extends the geometry of the soccer field and re-centers this west section of campus; and a new arrival space, a circle, shared by the Maryland Center for Performing Arts and the existing stadium.

The design for the MCPA itself utilizes a pattern of quadrangles in varying sizes and degrees of enclosure which identify entrances to the building and the primary departments. The main entrance courtyard is shared by the visiting public and the music library. Within the complex are separate music, dance, and theater courtyards that connect to and embrace the surrounding landscape.

In response to the site, the building is a mixture of three geometries relating to a public axis and interior street space: the orthogonal geometry of the campus; the angle of University Boulevard; and the angle of Stadium Drive. The geometries and volumes of the major performance spaces come together at the lobby space, conceived metaphorically as a medieval city street. The architectural result is a kind of village, a miniature campus of inter-connected structures. The largest performance space, over a hundred feet tall, is like the cathedral of a medieval town. The town metaphor is reinforced by multiple entrances for arriving and departing students and by the variety of interior and exterior courtyards and plazas. Student circulation is along a cross-axis linked with the public axis and extending through the major lobby space to the exterior courtyard, to dining, and to the outdoor amphitheater.

While Moore Ruble Yudell's winning competition scheme closely resembles the final project design for the Maryland Center for Performing Arts, the schematic design phase entailed not only a tedious process of program verification, but also retesting the initial design solution against other possible configurations. This led to important design changes and improvements in both the building and the site plan. As significant as these tests of the *parti* were, and as significant as the changes are for the final scheme, the basic design approach—the concept of the academic village—remained constant. The university's and jury's initial belief in Moore Ruble Yudell's open, flexible, and creative response to the client, and the architect's collaborative approach to the project, was confirmed throughout the schematic and design development phases of the project.

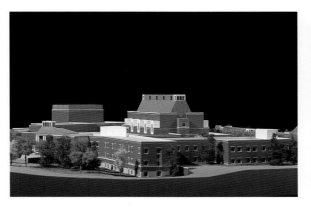

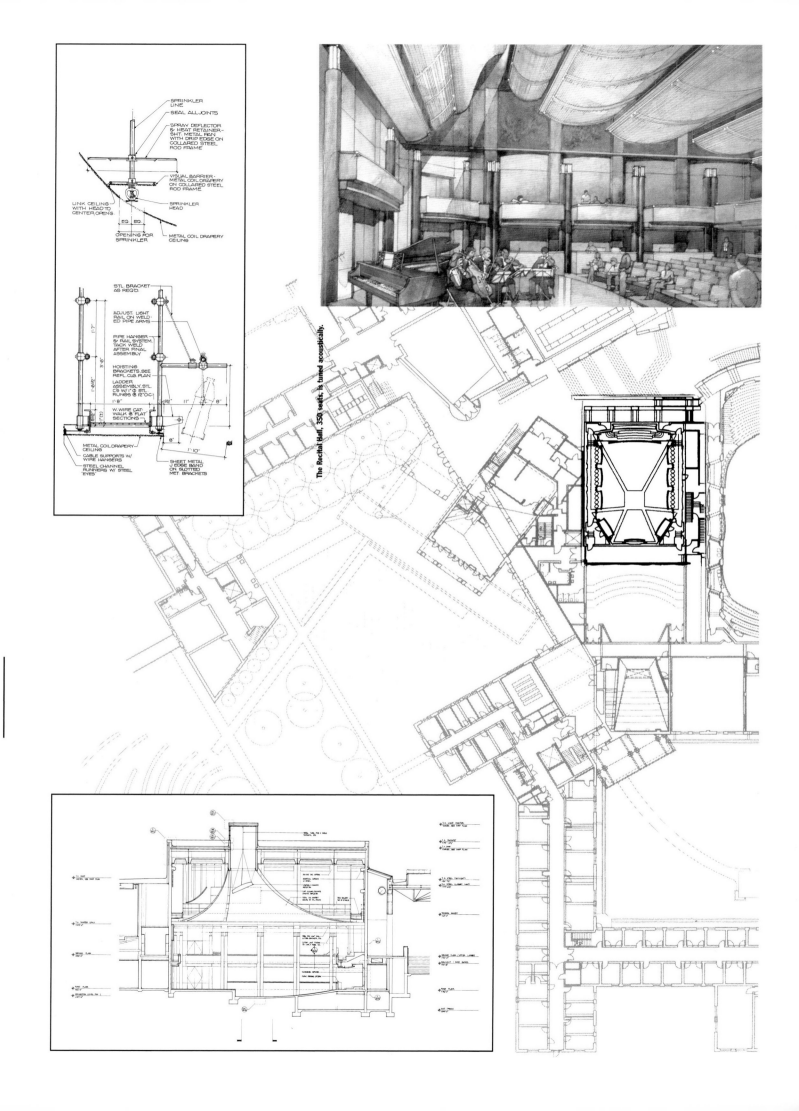

SPRINKLER
LINE

SEAL ALL JOINTS

SPRAY DEFLECTOR
& HEAT RETAINER-
SHT. METAL PAN
WITH DRIP EDGE ON
COLLARED STEEL
ROD FRAME

VISUAL BARRIER-
METAL COIL DRAPERY
ON COLLARED STEEL
ROD FRAME

LINK CEILING
WITH HEAD TO
CENTER OPENG.

SPRINKLER
HEAD

EQ   EQ

OPENING FOR
SPRINKLER

METAL COIL DRAPERY
CEILING

STL. BRACKET
AS REQ'D.

ADJUST. LIGHT
RAIL ON WELD-
ED PIPE ARMS

PIPE HANGER
& RAIL SYSTEM,
TACK WELD
AFTER FINAL
ASSEMBLY

HOISTING
BRACKETS, SEE
REFL. CLG. PLAN

LADDER
ASSEMBLY, STL.
C5 W/ 1" Ø STL.
RUNGS @ 12" O.C.

W. WIRE CAT-
WALK @ FLAT
SECTIONS.

METAL COIL DRAPERY
CEILING

CABLE SUPPORTS W/
WIRE HANGERS

STEEL CHANNEL
RUNNERS W/ STEEL
'EYES'

SHEET METAL
J EDGE BAND
ON SLOTTED
MET. BRACKETS

The Recital Hall, 350 seats, is tuned acoustically.

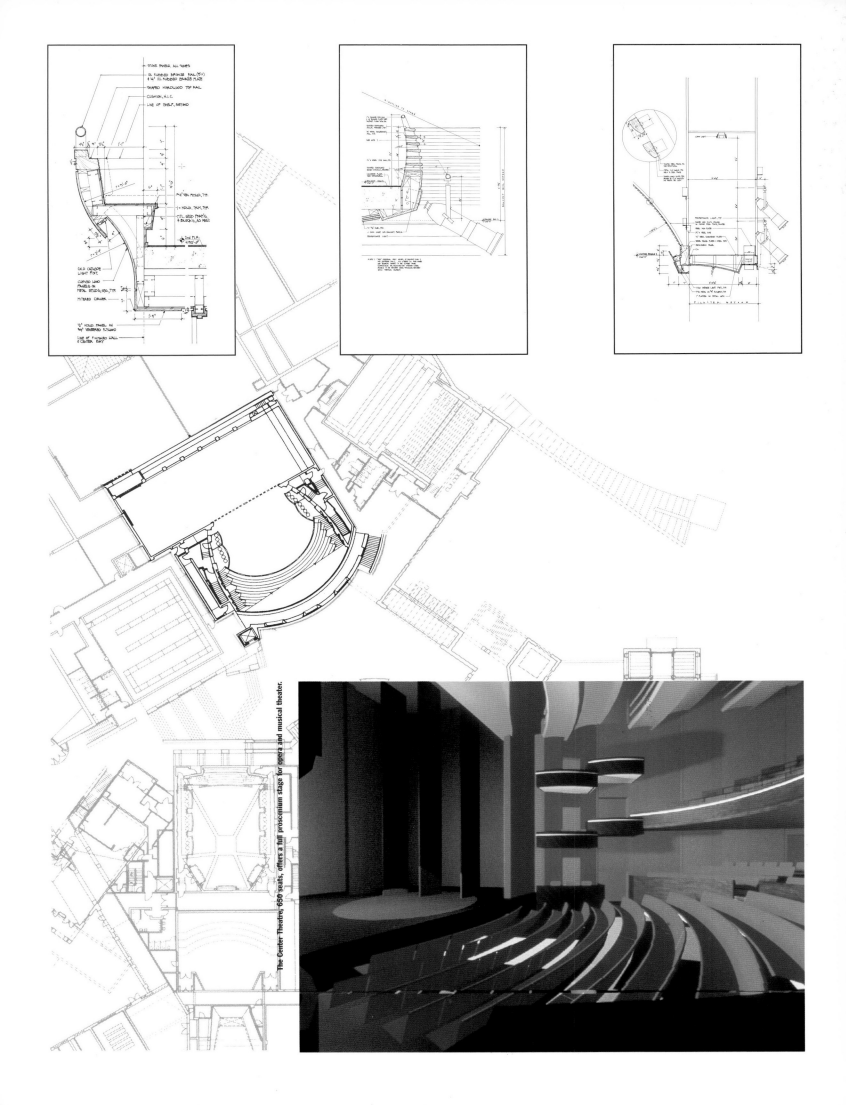

The Center Theatre, 650 seats, offers a full proscenium stage for opera and musical theater.

A model with the roofs of the central "street" removed shows the continuity from inside to outside.

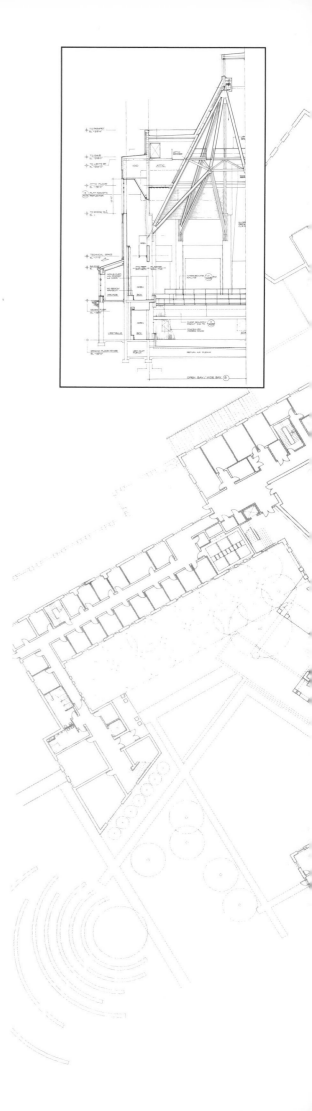

The play of natural and artificial light highlights the Concert Hall's trusswork canopy.

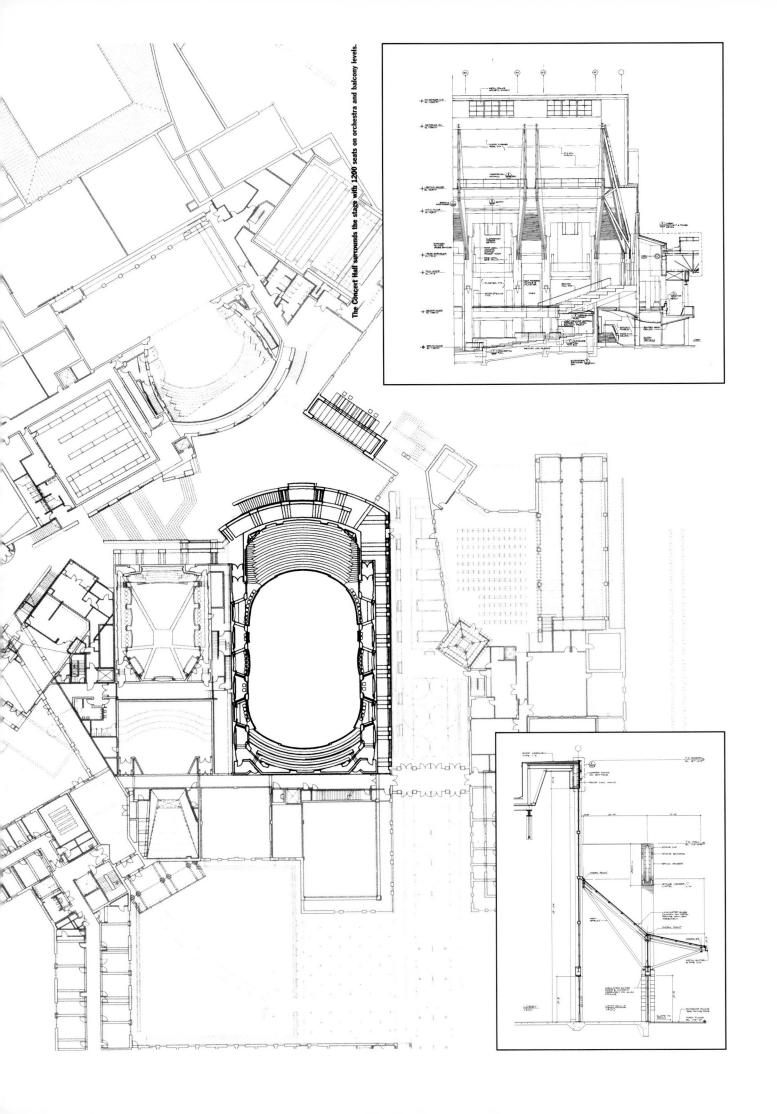

The Concert Hall surrounds the stage with 1200 seats on orchestra and balcony levels.

Moore Ruble Yudell's master plan for a new branch campus for the University of Washington encompasses a transitional hillside just south of downtown Tacoma, Washington. The 40-acre site includes a major portion of Tacoma's historic warehouse district, which has been neglected and largely dormant since the 1920s. It also encompasses a partially-abandoned residential area to the east, up a hillside, which at its crest offers commanding views of Tacoma Harbor, the surrounding city, and Mount Rainier in the distance. Because the University of Washington has until now had only one campus, there is a strong desire to fit this new branch campus into its context in a way that will foster a synergistic relationship between the university and the city. Moore Ruble Yudell's initial strategies have included a reinforcement of the existing street grid and existing frontages and building heights, and the preservation of view corridors throughout the upper site.

The first phase of the University of Washington Tacoma Campus will take advantage of the rich historic context within the lower portion of the site—most uses will be housed in renovated existing buildings. Along this denser, more urban area, judicious

Snoqualmie/Rainier/19th Street axes link existing landmarks on and off the Tacoma site.

TACOMA CAMPUS MASTER PLAN, UNIVERSITY OF WASHINGTON

Tacoma, Washington

new construction will reinforce the urban context and existing fabric of warehouse and other historic buildings. The heart of the new campus will be a large plaza at the intersection of Nineteenth Street and Pacific Avenue, facing the new State Historical Museum and the renovated Union Station, across Pacific. One boundary of this central campus plaza is made by a former power substation—designed in the early part of this century as a Greek Revival temple and oriented along an angled railroad right-of-way—which will be renovated as the reading room of the central campus library. Joined to new state-of-the-art library facilities, it will be a memorable campus landmark.

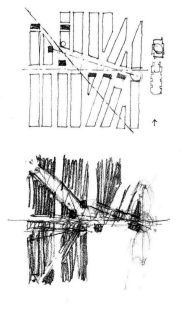

Early studies explore the movement up and down the sloping site.

Architect, Moore Ruble Yudell

Associate-in-Charge for the University of Washington Chemistry Building,

Tacoma Campus and University of California, Berkeley Walter A. Haas School of Business Administration

The memorable and enduring character of the greatest campuses and urban places of the world frequently stems from two particular attributes. First, they have a clear planning idea that makes them both unique and adaptable. Second, they have a strong sense of place, or "Genus Loci," as Christian Norberg-Schultz put it. The University of Washington Seattle Campus is an example of the perfect fusion of a spectacular place and a strong and flexible planning armature.

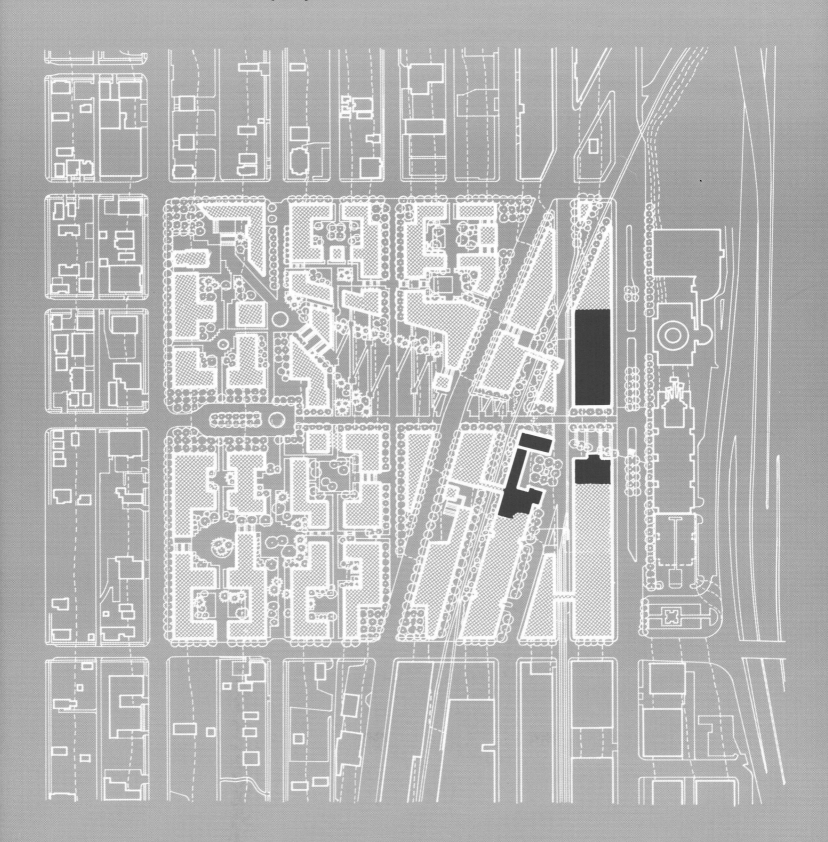

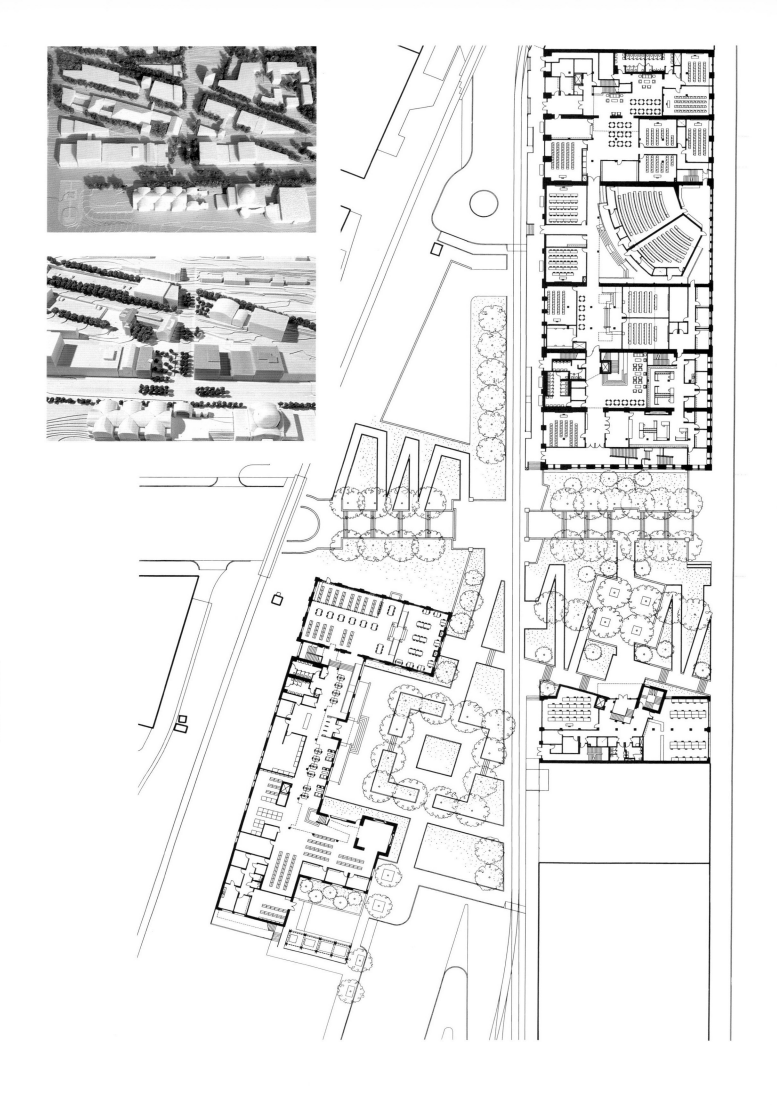

Splendid views to Mount Rainier and beyond, as well as the many fine (though partially derelict) 19th- and early-20th-century warehouses helped the University of Washington select the forty-acre site in downtown Tacoma for one of its two new branch campuses. Sloping steeply from east to west, the site gains a hundred feet of elevation over its full width. This means that as one ascends the site, panoramas across Mount Rainier, Puget Sound, and Tacoma's Commencement Bay, as well as the warehouses and Union Station, gradually come into view.

Further, the original urban street grid has undergone interesting modifications. Several angled streets and a rail line intersect the grid at approximately sixteen degrees, and one building—a gabled former electric power substation that is also the precinct's most monumental structure—is placed in alignment with this shifted orientation. The Beaux-Arts Union Station also stands adjacent to the site, designed by part of the team responsible for New York's Grand Central Terminal.

Moore Ruble Yudell was commissioned to design both a master plan for the general growth of the campus and a specific design for the first phase of building, to serve approximately 1,200 students. Taking cues from Seattle's main campus, the master plan was constructed as an overlay of the existing elements on the site, as well as a celebration of the regional views, in particular that of Mount Rainier. The existing grid of city blocks and much of the existing infrastructure of street rights-of-way and utilities will remain in place.

Three axes, identified for their present or future importance on the site, have been superimposed over this grid. One is the 19th Street center line, which divides the site equally between north and south. The second is suggested by the shifted urban grid, and the third is the sight line from the site's highest elevation to distant Mount Rainier.

The next site "overlay" includes three major, open squares to serve as arrival spaces at the east and west ends of the 19th Street axis, and as a central "green" at the heart of the campus. A series of up to six additional smaller open spaces are proposed for each city block, each serving as the focus for a different part of the campus.

To allow for incremental growth and change, a series of guidelines rather than a specific configuration is proposed. Critical formal aspects, such as the shaping of the three major open spaces, are controlled through the use of "build-to lines" that precisely define building dimensions and massing. Expanding toward the west, the major defining elements of the plan will be in place by the year 2010.

Now under construction, the first phase of the campus stretches from the predominantly commercial Pacific Avenue (a main Tacoma thoroughfare) to the right-of-way of the railroad (the first of the angled streets) and includes six renovated existing buildings and two new additions. Pacific Avenue will form a vital urban edge for the campus, with storefront spaces filled by retail uses oriented toward the student population. The next street up the hill, Commerce Street, meets the second-floor level of these revived warehouses and becomes the ground floor for campus functions and the main campus "street." The original warehouse loading docks will now serve as "front porches," with projecting canopies where students and faculty can congregate under cover from the often dramatic Pacific Northwest climate.

Architecturally, the existing buildings and their additions will retain as much of the rough-and-ready industrial character of the district as possible, inside and out. With vast interior spaces, the 120-foot-deep warehouses will each become an interior public gathering space at the ground level, opened up with skylit atria extending their entire four-story height. The existing heavy-timber construction will remain throughout. The library will be built around the restored power transformer substation, which will serve as its main reading room, and a new addition will house collections and staff spaces. As the campus grows, this building will form a link to the new campus precinct to the south.

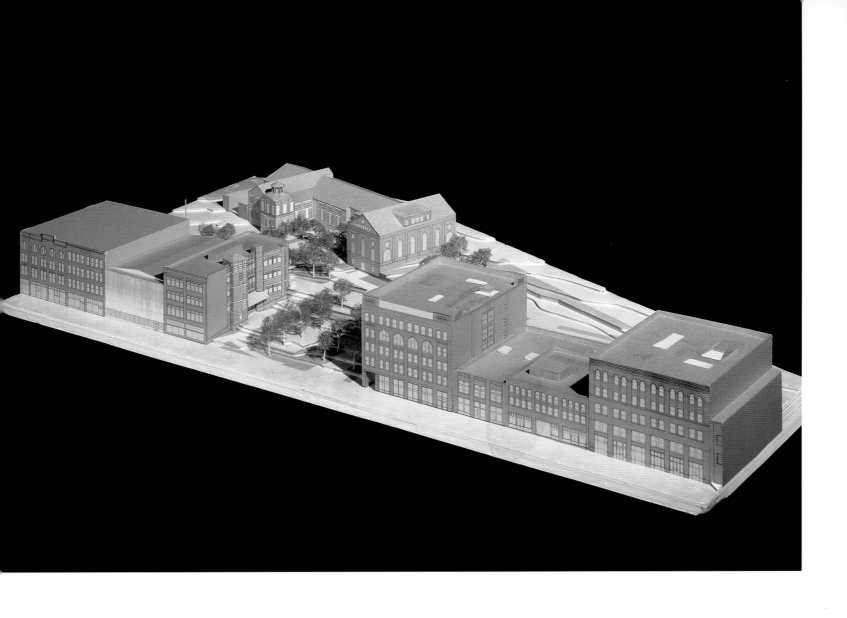

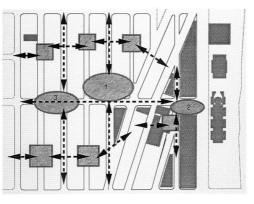

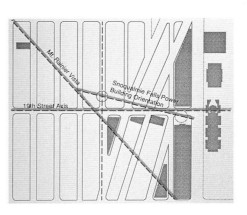

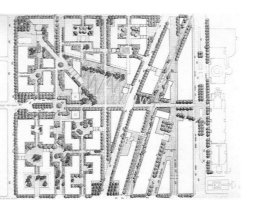

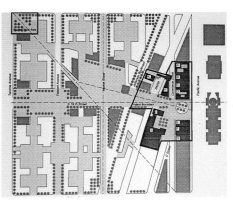

The campus library combines new construction with its main reading room in a renovated "Greek Temple" former power station to form a courtyard.

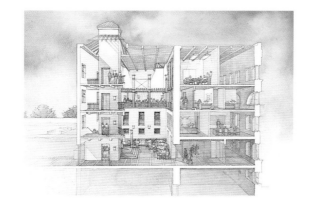

Infill construction includes a new central plaza and a new atrium within a renovated warehouse.

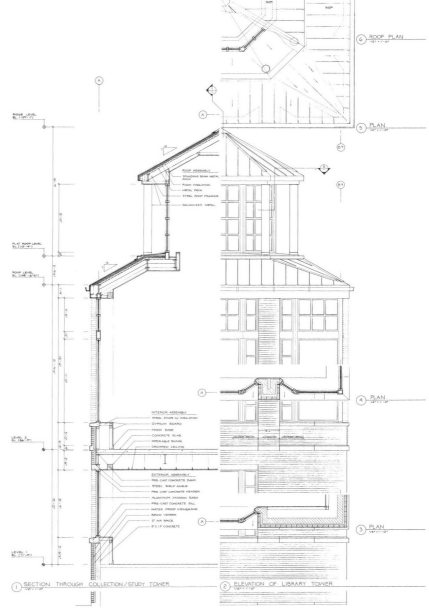

ROOF ASSEMBLY
STANDING SEAM METAL ROOF
RIGID INSULATION
METAL DECK
STEEL ROOF FRAMING
GALVANIZED METAL

INTERIOR ASSEMBLY
STEEL STUDS w/ INSULATION
GYPSUM BOARD
WOOD BASE
CONCRETE SLAB
OPERABLE SHADE
DROPPED CEILING

EXTERIOR ASSEMBLY
PRE-CAST CONCRETE BAND
STEEL SHELF ANGLE
PRE-CAST CONCRETE HEADER
ALUMINUM WINDOW SASH
PRE-CAST CONCRETE SILL
WATER PROOF MEMBRANE
BRICK VENEER
2" AIR SPACE
8" C.I.P. CONCRETE

RIDGE LEVEL
EL. (124'-1")

FLAT ROOF LEVEL
EL. (112'-4")

ROOF LEVEL
EL. (108'-6½")

LEVEL 2
EL. (86'-4")

LEVEL 1
EL. (71'-4")

1 SECTION THROUGH COLLECTION/STUDY TOWER
   1/2" = 1'-0"

2 ELEVATION OF LIBRARY TOWER
   1/2" = 1'-0"

3 PLAN
   1/2" = 1'-0"

4 PLAN
   1/2" = 1'-0"

5 PLAN
   1/2" = 1'-0"

6 ROOF PLAN
   1/2" = 1'-0"

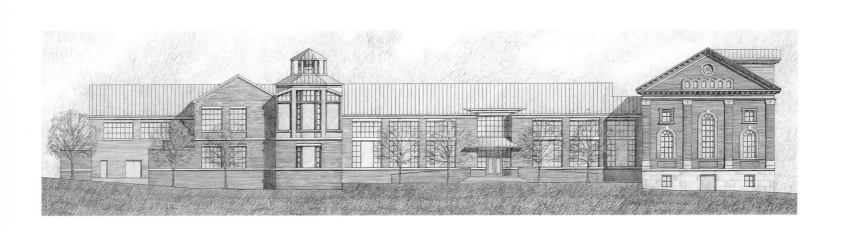

Comments on the Project by Tallman Trask

Executive Vice President, University of Washington

The University of Washington campus project in Tacoma couldn't be more different from our Seattle campus. The State of Washington ranks low in its participation rate in upper division higher education. To help rectify the problem, the state has embarked on an ambitious program of building a series of branch campuses, including one in Tacoma administered by the University of Washington.

Tacoma is an old industrial town, and most of its campus-like lands were long ago consumed by more intense uses. Finding a site wasn't easy. After much effort, my colleagues and I had begun to despair of finding an appropriate location. On a wet and windy morning, at the suggestion of some local business and political leaders, we finally took the rather radical step of looking for a site downtown.

What we found will be spectacular: nearly a dozen-turn-of-the-century (largely vacant) warehouses, highlighted by the Snoqualmie Falls Power Station. I took one look at it and knew that it was destined to be a library reading room. After much thought and study, Moore Ruble Yudell agreed to plan the new campus. By renovating the historic structures and infilling with only modest new construction, we will create a campus with an instant sense of history and place. If the schematic design turns out to be nearly as good as we think it is, the University of Washington will soon have two of the most remarkable campuses in the country.

Moore Ruble Yudell was asked to participate in a limited competition for the Grand Opera House, a major new cultural facility within the historic commercial center of Shanghai. Like other Chinese cities, Shanghai is enjoying an explosion of development as it struggles with new concepts of historic preservation of its urban fabric. This city, in particular, is an astonishing collection of Chinese-European hybrid buildings built over the last few centuries by immigrant communities. Its position at the mouth of the Yangtze River has given it a traditionally cosmopolitan air and a central importance as a Chinese port, and destination for the provinces along the river.

The site is located at one side of a large park, adjacent to the new City Hall and other proposed civic buildings. The park is the past site of the Shanghai race track, which was a social catalyst of some distinction, and several of the old, brick, fairground buildings remain.

Moore Ruble Yudell's scheme gathers these old buildings into a new complex in the tradition of Chinese courtyard typologies. The extensive program was broken down into separate theater

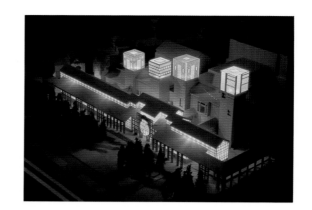

SHANGHAI GRAND THEATRE DESIGN

Shanghai, People's Republic of China

buildings, surrounded by an articulated wall of arcaded galleries and support buildings. There are three major theater/concert halls: a two-thousand-seat, European-style opera house, a medium-sized, flexible-seating hall (which can make the high-tech transformation from Elizabethan to Chinese courtyard theater), and a smaller, open-seating recital hall. This last opens through large, rolling doors to an outdoor garden with additional seating and stage areas. A continuous outdoor arcade gives shelter and shade along the street edge of the collection of buildings.

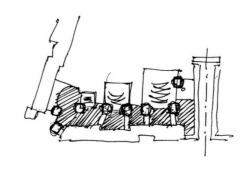

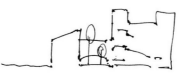

Shanghai Grand Theatre's lobby garden suggests a transition from daily life to the poet's world of imagination.

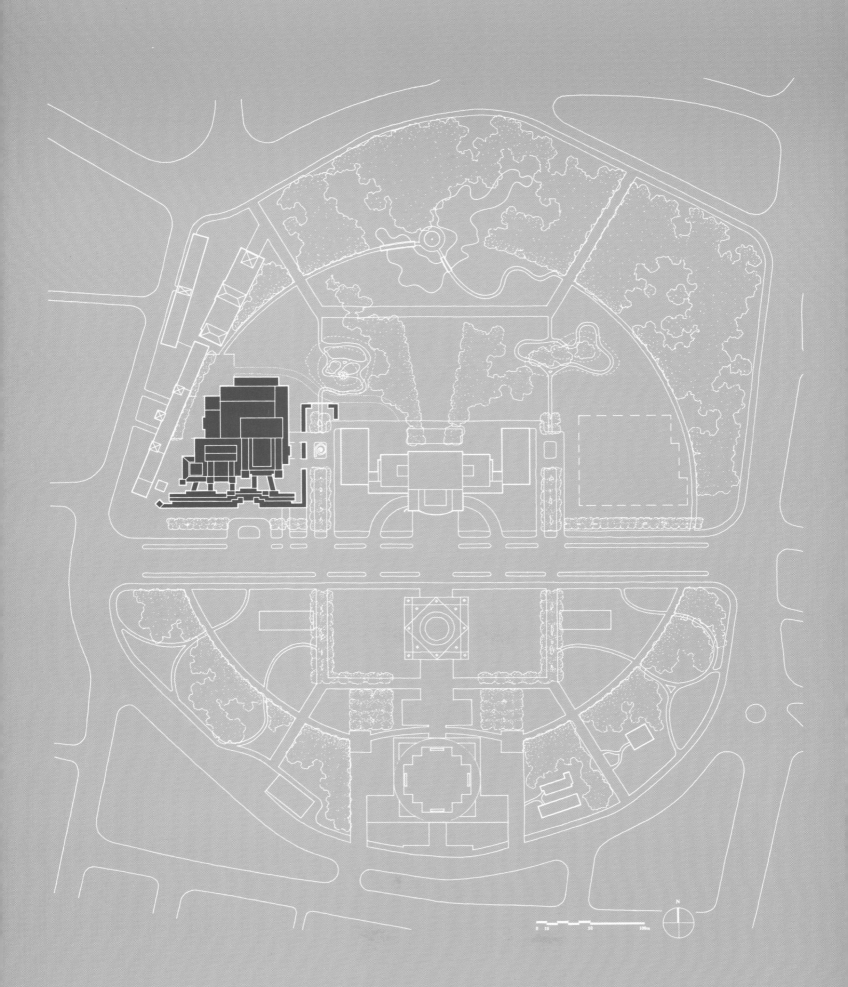

The most dramatic space is the four-hundred-foot-long glazed gallery that runs along the entire street edge of the complex, incorporating theater lobbies, reception halls, ticket offices, bars, and bookstores. Roofed in yellow-ochre tiles and with an undulating interior vault of brightly painted wood lattice, this grand promenade unites the exuberant massing of the theaters into a single memorable image. A limestone and terra-cotta screen lines the outdoor arcade, ending in a great lantern-like stone gateway at the main public entrance. An integral porte-cochère to one side allows VIPs to slip in quietly. The arcade continues past another small garden court to a moon-gate entrance to the park beyond.

Each theater entrance is a dramatic event. The three halls are entered by bridges that cross over a narrow, Chinese-inspired garden bordering the long gallery. The garden is in continuous transformation along its length, with a connecting stream curling past stone towers that mark the theater's entrances and circulation. The unexpected juxtaposition of grand gallery and intimate garden surprises the visitor and marks the transition from the public sphere to the heightened theatrical reality to come.

The theaters themselves are state-of-the-art, with the opera house containing a generous back-of-house area modeled after the Paris Opera. The two smaller theaters provide for enormous flexibility and creativity in alternative stagings and concerts.

Lighting has been incorporated into the building's massing, in the form of large-scale lanterns atop each tower, with decorative metal shrouds. Rising from behind the great glass gallery, these beacons join with other landmark towers in the central city to enliven the existing skyline and place this new world-class facility in the Shanghai cultural landscape.

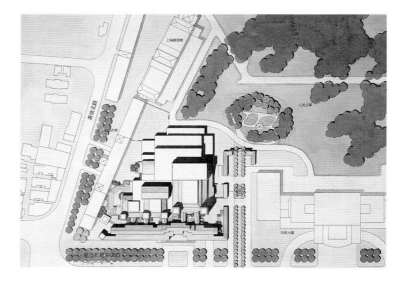

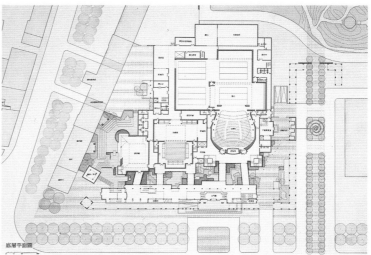

The grand axial lobby connects to performance halls across garden courtyards.

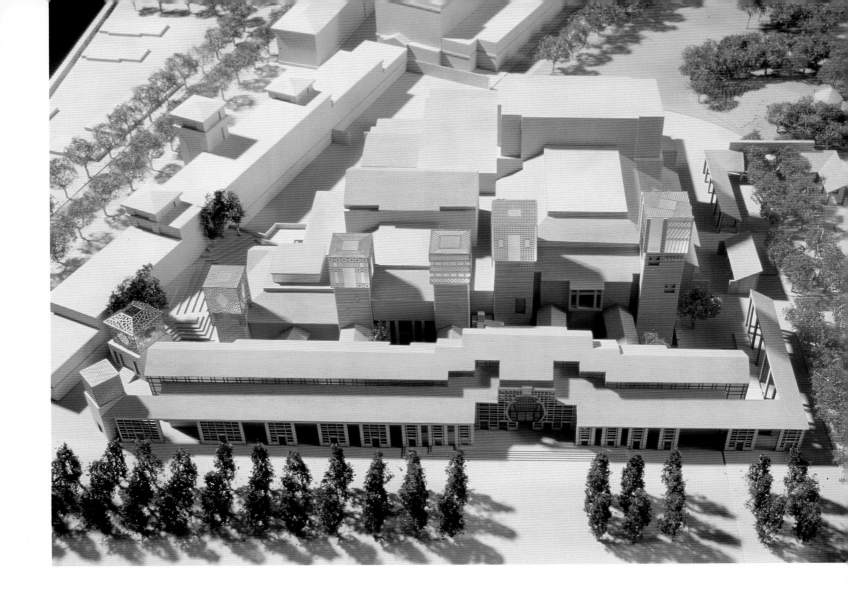

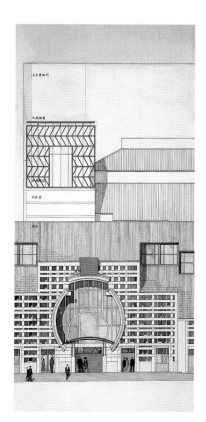

Light radiates through a stone lattice at the main entrance and a series of lanterns above.

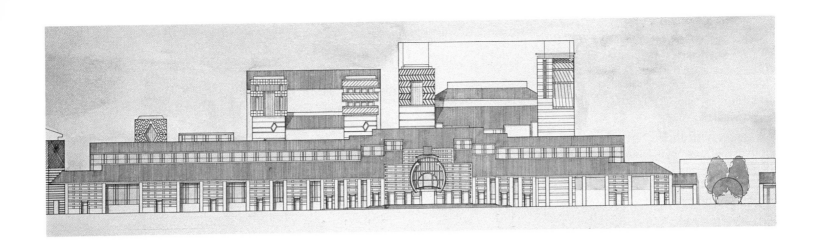

The three performance halls are diverse in size and character.

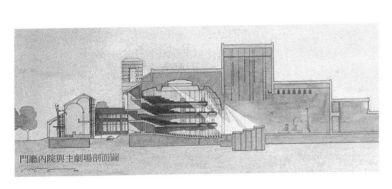

門廳內院與主劇場剖面圖

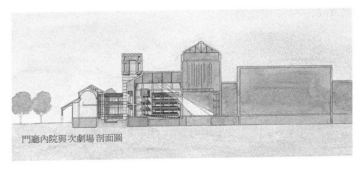

門廳內院與次劇場 剖面圖

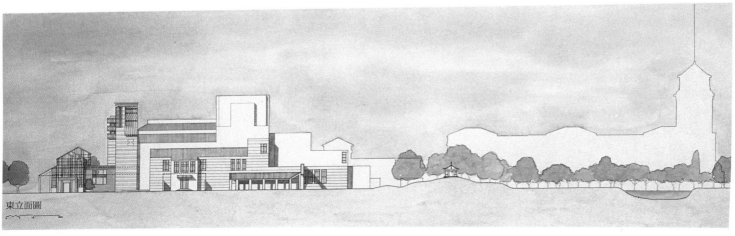

東立面圖

A fertile valley between the coastal and central mountains of Taiwan is the site for this new university campus. Eight undergraduate and graduate schools including engineering, arts, and sciences will accommodate more than one thousand faculty members, five hundred staff members, and ten thousand students. Moore Ruble Yudell's master plan juxtaposes an axis—oriented to the mountains—against a meandering water park of connected ponds and lakes. Inspired by river deltas near the site, the water park activates and complements the formal geometries of the plan and recalls the classic use of water to delineate the boundaries of palaces and temple complexes throughout Asia.

In the central campus, the library, administration, and other pan-university uses occupy sites along the main axis flanked by courtyard complexes that house individual schools. The courtyards provide an outdoor social heart for each school and also serve to shelter trees from frequent typhoons. Faculty and student housing, theaters, sports, and community facilities are sited along the water, which widens to mark special places (the central plaza, the student union) and doubles as a key element in the system of campus flood control.

DONG-HWA NATIONAL UNIVERSITY CAMPUS MASTER PLAN

Hwa-Lien, Taiwan

Moore Ruble Yudell's work as master planners has focused on design of the overall campus infrastructure, public space, and landscape, with extensive design and color guidelines to establish a context for individual buildings. Influences of culture and climate are expressed in broad, tree-shaded boulevards and playfully spirited bridges, which celebrate the daily movements of students as they bicycle to and from residences and classes.

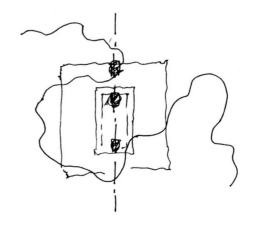

A hierachical set of precincts is traversed by a connected string of ponds and lakes.

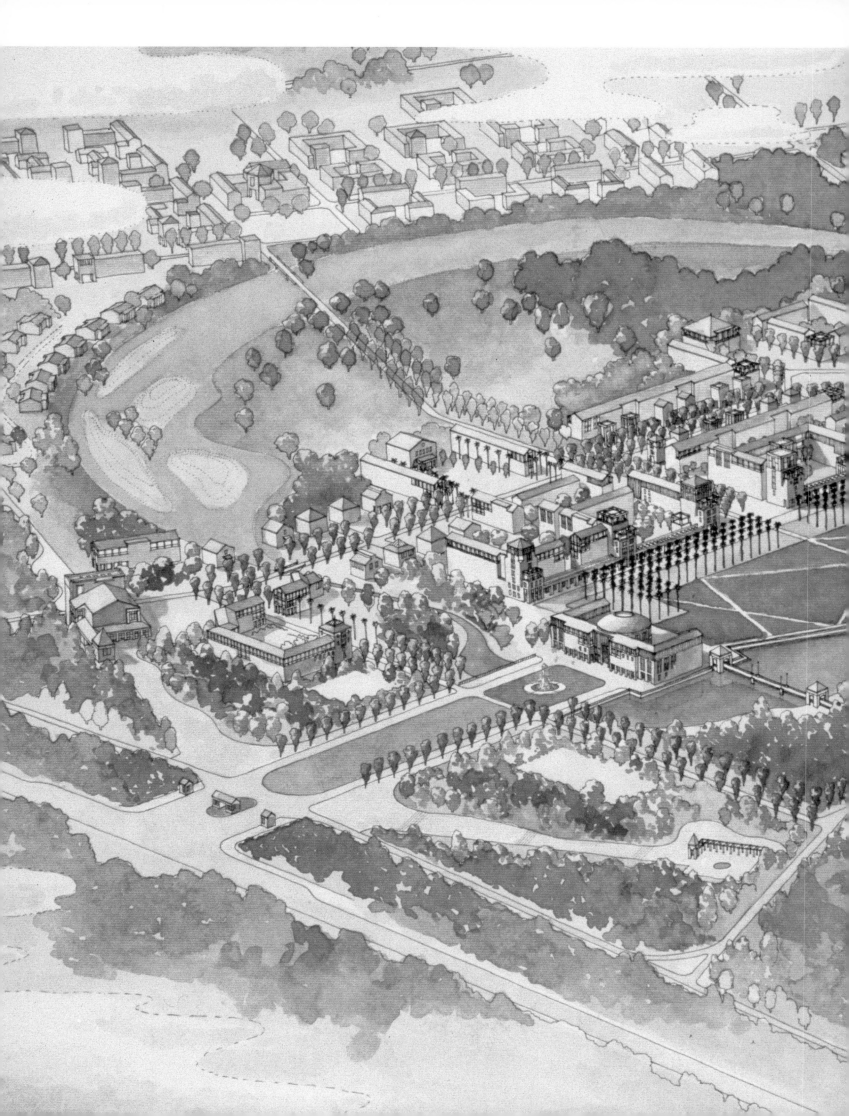

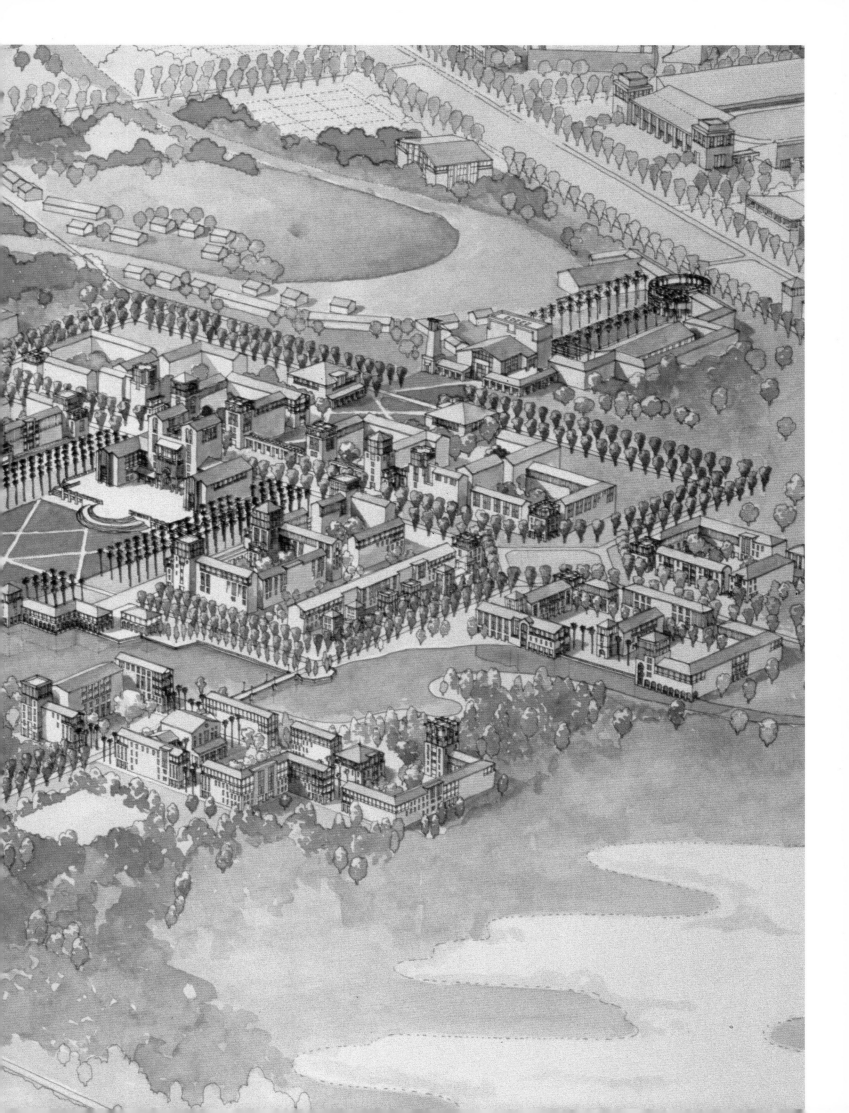

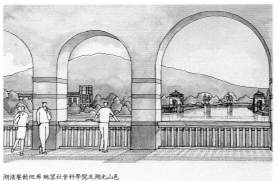

湖濱餐飲迎麻 眺望社會科學院及湖光山色
WING TOWARD SCHOOL OF SOCIAL SCIENCE AND NATURAL SCENERY FROM LAKE FRONT CAFETERIA

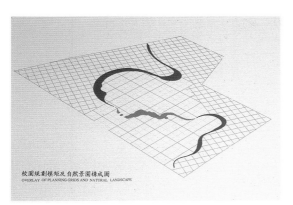
土地使用分析圖
ZONING DIAGRAM

景觀及植栽規劃
LANDSCAPE DIAGRAM

校園規劃模矩及自然景園構成圖
OVERLAY OF PLANNING GRIDS AND NATURAL LANDSCAPE

校園分期分區發展構想
PHASING AND EXPANSION

The master plan suggests a hierarchical layering of architectural spaces.

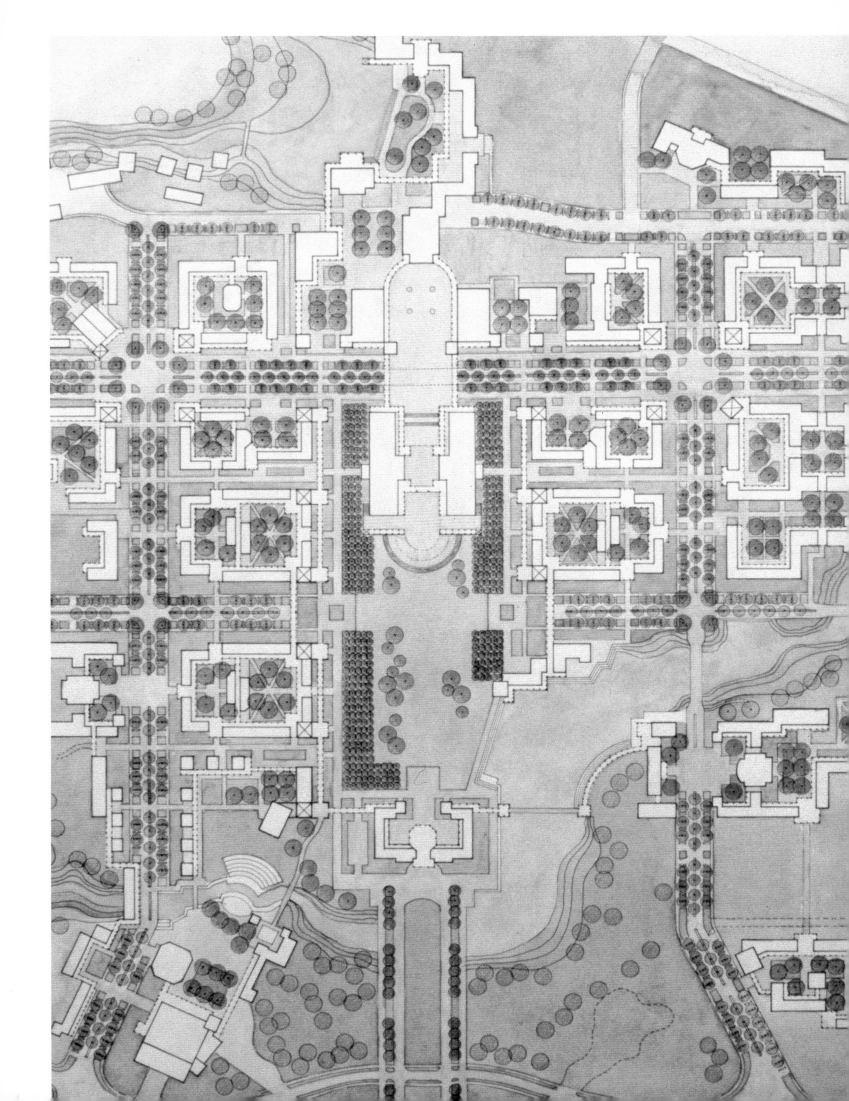

As the campus takes shape, a variety of architects will contribute to its character.

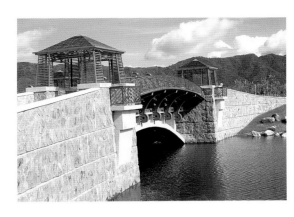

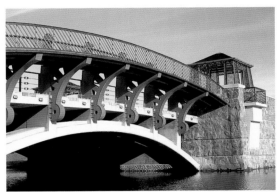

Moore Ruble Yudell designed bridges and other components of the infrastructure.

A new technological institute with four related schools, faculty and student housing, and sports facilities is located close to the industrial city of Kao-Shiung on the south-west coast of Taiwan. Moore Ruble Yudell's master plan works within the constraints of the site, including a major highway that splits the site in two, to create a richly articulated campus. The design unites the divided site by establishing a graceful, curved main pedestrian mall that links the two sides, one primarily for housing and recreation, the other for academic and administration buildings. The link over the highway—a broad pedestrian bridge—also serves as a symbolic gateway for motorists. The pedestrian mall is animated by open plazas at various points, such as the student union and lecture hall square. The main library and baseball stadium serve to anchor the sequence at either end. The Institute's administration building serves as a focal point for a major "green" cross-axis on the academic side. Faculty residences are arranged around a radial park that embraces the main library. Vehicular and service access is provided by a loop road throughout the site.

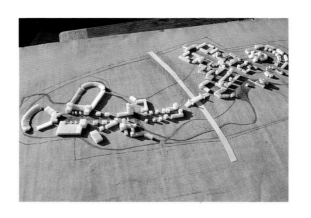

KAO-SHIUNG NATIONAL INSTITUTE OF TECHNOLOGY
CAMPUS MASTER PLAN DESIGN

Kao-Shiung, Taiwan

Both halves of the campus are entered from the south, with the major entry leading to the academic area. Throughout the campus, arcades along the buildings offer shade and lend a cohesive pattern to the whole, while school buildings create courtyards to provide natural ventilation in Taiwan's humid, harsh, and often stormy climate. Strategically placed towers—such as a pair around the dormitory square—act as points of orientation. A picturesque stream winds through the site and into a quiet lake adjacent to the administration building, enhancing the lyrical, poetic qualities of the plan.

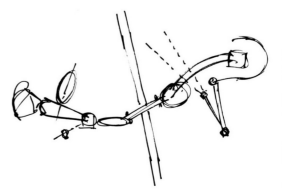

An event-filled procession links a divided site.

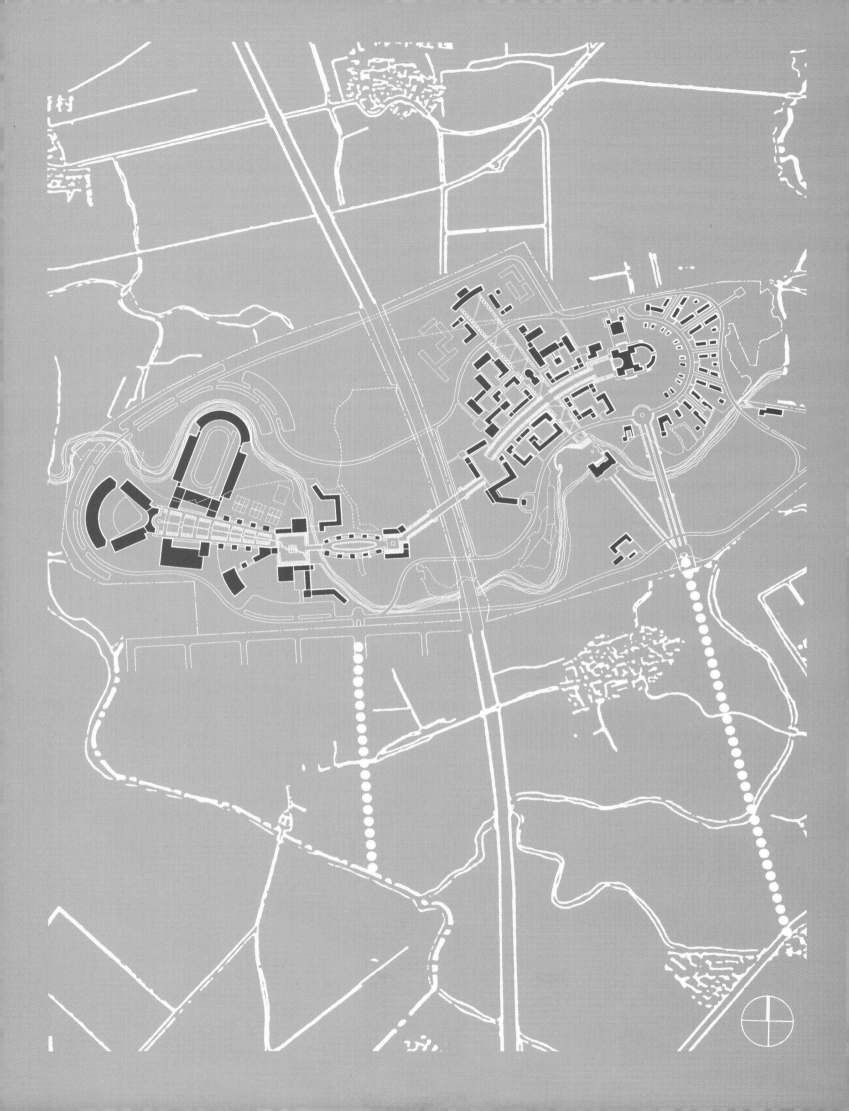

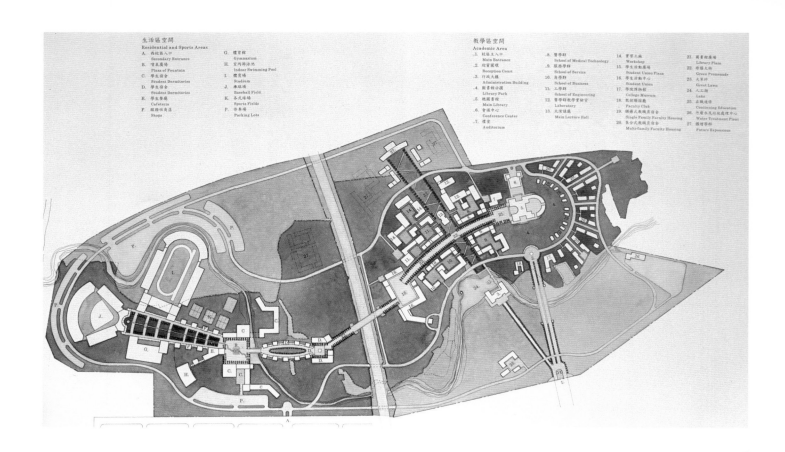

生活區空間
Residential and Sports Areas

A. 西紋區入口
   Secondary Entrance
B. 噴泉廣場
   Plaza of Fountain
C. 學生宿舍
   Student Dormitories
D. 學生宿舍
   Student Dormitories
E. 學生餐廳
   Cafeteria
F. 服務性商店
   Shops

G. 體育館
   Gymnasium
H. 室內游泳池
   Indoor Swimming Pool
I. 體育場
   Stadium
J. 棒球場
   Baseball Field
K. 各式球場
   Sports Fields
P. 停車場
   Parking Lots

教學區空間
Academic Area

1. 校務主入口
   Main Entrance
2. 迎賓園環
   Reception Court
3. 行政大樓
   Administration Building
4. 圖書總公園
   Library Park
5. 總圖書館
   Main Library
6. 會議中心
   Conference Center
7. 禮堂
   Auditorium

8. 醫學群
   School of Medical Technology
9. 服務學群
   School of Service
10. 商學群
    School of Business
11. 工學群
    School of Engineering
12. 醫學群教學實驗室
    Laboratory
13. 大演講廳
    Main Lecture Hall

14. 實習工廠
    Workshop
15. 學生活動廣場
    Student Union Plaza
16. 學生活動中心
    Student Union
17. 學院博物館
    College Museum
18. 教授聯誼館
    Faculty Club
19. 獨棟式教職員宿舍
    Single Family Faculty Housing
20. 公寓式教職員宿舍
    Multi-family Faculty Housing

21. 圖書館廣場
    Library Plaza
22. 綠蔭大道
    Green Promenade
23. 大草坪
    Great Lawn
24. 人工湖
    Lake
25. 公職進修
    Continuing Education
26. 行政作業處理中心
    Water Treatment Plant
27. 預預學群
    Future Expansions

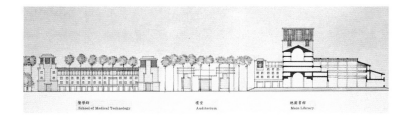

School of Medical Technology   禮堂 Auditorium   總圖書館 Main Library

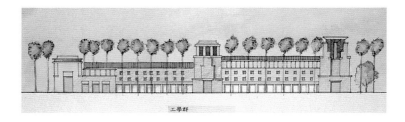

工學群

Integrated systems of circulation, open space, axial views, and building form unify academic and residential precincts across an existing highway.

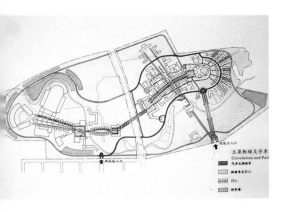

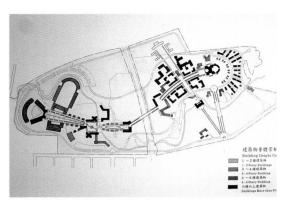

建築物量體管制
Building Height Co...
1 - 2層建築物
1 - 2 Storey Buildings
3 - 4層建築物
3 - 4 Storey Building
4 - 6層建築物
4 - 6 Storey Building
六層以上建築物
Buildings More than 6...

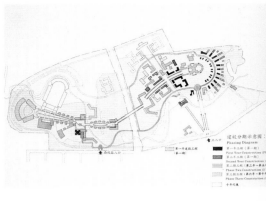

建築分期示意圖
Phasing Diagram
第一年之道路工程
First Year Construction
第二年工程
Second Year Construction (Ph...
第二期三期工程(第一期)
Phase Two Construction (2 St...
第三期工程(第六年~第十年)
Phase Three Construction (3...

主要綠帶配置圖
Major Green Zones

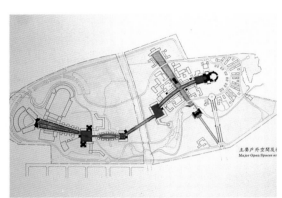

主要戶外空間及...
Major Open Spaces ar...

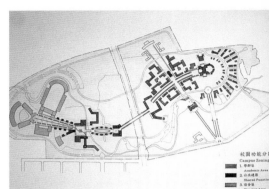

校園功能分區...
Campus Zoning F...
1. 學群區
Academic Area
2. 公共建築
Shared Function
3. 宿舍區
Housing Area

醫學科   服務學科   人工湖   行政大樓
School of Medical Technology   School of Service   Lake   Administration Building

APPENDIX

PROJECT CREDITS

UNIVERSITY OF OREGON SCIENCE COMPLEX

Principal-in-Charge: Buzz Yudell
Principal Designers: Charles Moore, John Ruble, Buzz Yudell
Project Architects: Stephen Harby, Jim Morton
Project Team: Hong Chen, Neal Matsuno, Bill Mochidome, William Murray, George Nakatani, James Mary O'Connor, Patrick Ousey, Richard Song, Renzo Zecchetto, Brian Tichenor, Katie Zobal
Executive Architect: The Ratcliff Architects, Kit Ratcliff, Christie Coffin, Carl Christianson, Stefanie Bartos, Tak Yamamoto, David Alpert
Associate Architect: Brockmeyer McDonnell
Laboratory Consultant: McLellan & Copenhagen
Lighting: Richard C. Peters
Landscape: Royston, Hanamoto, Alley & Abey, Cameron & McCarthy
Arts Administrator: Lotte Streisinger
Artists: Kent Bloomer, Ed Carpenter, Wayne Chabre, Jane Marquis, Ken Von Roenn, Alice Wingwall, Scott Wylie
Color: Tina Beebe

SAN ANTONIO ART INSTITUTE

Principal-in-Charge: Buzz Yudell
Principal Designers: Charles Moore, John Ruble, Buzz Yudell
Project Architect: Renzo Zecchetto
Project Manager, Schematic Design Phase: Miguel Escobar
Head of Production: Alfeo B. Diaz
Project Team: Hong Chen, George Nakatani, Paul Nagashima, James Mary O'Connor, Erik Mikiten, Steve Vitalich
Renderings: James Mary O'Connor

HUMBOLDT BIBLIOTHEK

Principal-in-Charge: John Ruble
Principal Designers: Charles Moore, John Ruble, Buzz Yudell
Project Manager: Thomas Nagel
Project Team: Leon Glodt, Regina Pizzinini, Renzo Zecchetto
Consulting Architect: Walter Hötzel
Associate Architect: Abeln, Lubic, Skoda
Color: Tina Beebe

PETER BOXENBAUM ARTS EDUCATION CENTER

Principal-in-Charge: Buzz Yudell
Principal Designers: Charles Moore, John Ruble, Buzz Yudell
Project Manager: Leon Glodt
Project Team: Daniel Garness, Miguel Escobar, Alfeo B. Diaz, Hong Chen
Lighting: Richard C. Peters
Color: Tina Beebe

UCSD CELLULAR AND MOLECULAR MEDICINE EAST & WEST

WEST WING
Principal-in-Charge: John Ruble
Principal Designers: Charles Moore, John Ruble, Buzz Yudell
Project Architects: Markku Kari, Michael de Villiers
Project Team: James Mary O'Connor, Akai Ming-Kae Yang
Associate Architect: The Ratcliff Architects
Laboratory Consultants: Research Facilities Design
Lighting: Richard C. Peters
Artwork: Jackie Ferrara
Landscape: The Spurlock Office
Color: Tina Beebe
EAST WING
Principal-in-Charge: John Ruble
Principal Designers: Charles Moore, John Ruble, Buzz Yudell
Associate-in-Charge: David Kaplan
Project Team: Steve Gardner, Richard Destin, Christopher Kenney, Ying-Chao Kuo
Model Makers: John Taft, Craig Currie
Associate Architect: Lee, Burkhart, Liu
Landscape: The Spurlock Office
Mechanical Consultant: Store, Metakovitch, Wolfberg
Laboratory Consultants: McClellan and Copenhegan
Color: Tina Beebe

WALTER A. HAAS SCHOOL OF BUSINESS ADMINISTRATION

Principal-in-Charge: John Ruble
Principal Designers: Charles Moore, John Ruble, Buzz Yudell
Associate-in-Charge: Stephen Harby
Project Architect: Chris Kenney
Project Team: Steve Gardner, Anton Vetterlein, Markku Kari, Angel Gabriel, Brian Tichenor, Mark Denton, Daniel Garness, James Mary O'Connor
Model Makers: John Taft, Arnold Swanborn
Renderings: Al Forster
Associate Architect: VBN Corporation, Franz Steiner, Dan Odasz, William Lyons, I. K. Cha, Harold Hayashi, Tom Saxby
Landscape: Arbegast, Newton and Griffith
Lighting: Peters & Myer
Color: Tina Beebe

CALIFORNIA CENTER FOR THE ARTS, ESCONDIDO

Principal-in-Charge: Buzz Yudell
Principal Designers: Charles Moore, John Ruble, Buzz Yudell
Project Director: Jim Morton
Project Architect: Renzo Zecchetto
Site Architect, Project Manager, Conference Center: Denise Haradem
Project Manager, Community Theatre: Hong Chen
Project Manager, Art Center: George Nakatani
Project Manager, Lyric Theatre: Martin Saavedra
Project Manager, Site Development: Neal Matsuno
Head of Production: Alfeo B. Diaz
Project Team: Linda Brettler, Camillo Carillo, Richard Destin, Ted Elayda, Angel Gabriel, Steve Gardner, John Johnson, Rebecca Kaplan, Shuji Kurokawa, Wing-Hon Ng, Jesse Marcial, Cynthia Phakos, Geoffrey Siebens, Tony Tran, Gene Treadwell, Duk-Hwan Lee, Heather Trossman, George Venini, Ric Tayag, Tony Reyes
Building Systems Consultant: Ove Arup and Partners, California
Theatre Consultant: Theatre Projects Consultants
Acoustician: The Talaske Group Inc.
Interiors: Audrey Alberts
Landscape: Burton and Spitz
Color: Tina Beebe

UNIVERSITY OF WASHINGTON CHEMISTRY BUILDING

Principal-in-Charge: John Ruble
Principal Designers: Charles Moore, John Ruble, Buzz Yudell
Associate-in-Charge: Stephen Harby
Project Architect: Chris Kenney
Programming and Workshops Coordinator: Mark Denton
Project Team: Sylvia Deily, Ying-Chao Kuo, Wendy Kohn, Yvonne Yao, Julie Malork
Associate Architect: Loschky, Marquardt & Nesholm, John Nesholm, Rich Wilson, Dean Clark, George Shaw, Alan Worthington
Laboratory Planner: McLellan & Copenhagen
Mechanical Consultant: Affiliated Engineers Inc.
Landscape: Murase Associates
Color: Tina Beebe

POWELL LIBRARY RENOVATION, UC LOS ANGELES

Principal-in-Charge: Buzz Yudell
Principal Designers: John Ruble, Buzz Yudell
Project Architect: Michael de Villiers
Project Team: Martin Saavedra, Jeanne Chen, Neal Matsuno, Angel Gabriel, Wing-Hon Ng, Alfeo B. Diaz, Stephen Harby, Ying-Chao Kuo, Mary Beth Elliott, Daniel Garness, George Nakatani, Bill Murray, Bob Meiklejohn, Gene Treadwell, Wendy Kohn, Jim Morton
Color: Tina Beebe

THE HUGH AND HAZEL DARLING LAW LIBRARY ADDITION

Principal-in-Charge: Buzz Yudell
Principal Designers: John Ruble, Buzz Yudell
Associate-in-Charge: Stephen Harby
Project Architect: Jeanne Chen
Project Team: Don Aitken, Bob Anderson, Alfeo B. Diaz, Mary Beth Elliot, Angel Gabriel, Florence Huang, Neal Matsuno, Wing-Hon Ng, Adam Padua, Ric Tayag, Tony Tran, Gene Treadwell, Akai Ming-Kae Yang
Model Makers: Mark Grand, Craig Currie, Chris Roades
Landscape: Pamela Burton & Co.
Color: Tina Beebe
Interiors: Audrey Alberts

AVERY HOUSE, CALIFORNIA INSTITUTE OF TECHNOLOGY

Principal-in-Charge: Buzz Yudell
Principal Designers: John Ruble, Buzz Yudell
Associate-in-Charge: Mark Denton
Competition Team: Mark Denton, James Mary O'Connor, David Kaplan, Steve Gardner
Project Architect: Linda Brettler
Head of Production: Alfeo B. Diaz
Project Team: Richard Destin, Roger Lopez, Rudy Modina, James Jackson, Michael Xu, Carlos Cruz, Tony Tran, Tony Reyes, Martin Saavedra
Landscape: Pamela Burton
Color: Tina Beebe

MARYLAND CENTER FOR PERFORMING ARTS

COMPETITION
Principal-in-Charge: Buzz Yudell
Principal Designers: John Ruble, Buzz Yudell
Associate-in-Charge: Jim Morton
Project Architect: James Mary O'Connor
Project Team: Celina Welch, Bob Anderson, Erica Moon, Daniel Garness, Shuji Kurokawa, Akai Ming-Kae Yang, Mark Peacor, Tony Tran, Mario Violich, Adrian Koffka, Adam Padua
Renderings: Al Forster, Daniel Garness
PROJECT DESIGN
Principal-in-Charge: Buzz Yudell
Principal Designers: John Ruble, Buzz Yudell
Associate-in-Charge: Jim Morton
Project Architect: James Mary O'Connor
Project Administrator: Harry Steinway
Project Manager for Performance Areas: Hong Chen
Project Manager for Academic Areas: Denise Haradem
Technical Manager: Martin Saavedra
CAD Manager: Mary Jane Kopitzke
Head of Production: Alfeo B. Diaz
Project Team: Erica Moon, Bob Anderson, Adam Padua, Kaz Baba, Wendy Kohn, Akai Ming-Kae Yang, Richard Williams, Amy Alper, Holly Bieniewski, Michael Xu, Christine Cho, Thurman Grant, Mary Beth Elliott, Sara Loe, Angel Gabriel, Tony Tran
Model Maker: Chris Roades
Color: Tina Beebe
Associated Architect: Ayers/Saint/Gross Architects, Richard Ayers, Adam Gross, George Thomas, Duncan Kirk, John Dale, Peter Garver.
Landscape Architect: Michael Vergason
Theatre Consultants: Theatre Projects Consultants Inc.
Acoustical Consultants: R. Lawrence Kirkegaard and Associates
Interiors: Audrey Alberts

TACOMA CAMPUS MASTER PLAN, UNIVERSITY OF WASHINGTON

Principal-in-Charge: John Ruble
Principal Designers: Charles Moore, John Ruble, Buzz Yudell
Associate-In-Charge: Stephen Harby
Project Architects: Steve Gardner, Michael de Villiers
Project Team: Gene Treadwell, Richard Williams, Tony Reyes, Oli Florendo, Chris Kenney, Erica Moon, David Kaplan, Neal Matsuno, Angel Gabriel, Ric Tayag, Wendy Kohn, Tony Tran
Model Makers: Mark Grand, Florence Huang, Tony Pritchard
Renderings: Al Forster
Associate Architects: Loschky Marquardt and Nesholm

SHANGHAI GRAND THEATRE DESIGN

Principal-in-Charge: John Ruble
Principal Designers: John Ruble, Buzz Yudell
Associate-in-Charge: Daniel Garness
Project Team: Adrian Koffka, Marc Schoeplein, Wendy Kohn, Adam Padua, Tony Tran, Steve Gardner, Wing-Hon Ng, Mario Violich
Renderings: Al Forster
Color: Tina Beebe
Project Liason: Eddie Lee

DONG-HWA UNIVERSITY MASTER PLAN

Principal-in-Charge: John Ruble
Principal Designers: Charles Moore, John Ruble, Buzz Yudell
Associate-in-Charge: Akai Ming-Kae Yang
Project Architect: Ying-Chao Kuo
Associated Architect: LAI Associates
Project Team: George Nakatani, Marc Peacor
Model Makers: Craig Currie, Mark Grand
Rendering: George Nakatani

KAO-SHIUNG NATIONAL INSTITUTE OF TECHNOLOGY CAMPUS MASTER PLAN DESIGN

Principal-in-Charge: John Ruble
Principal Designers: Charles Moore, John Ruble, Buzz Yudell
Associate-in-Charge: Akai Ming-Kae Yang
Project Architect: James Mary O'Connor
Project Team: Celina Welch, Erica Moon, Mario Violich, Tony Tran, Wing-Hon Ng, John Johnson
Renderings: James Mary O'Connor, Mario Violich

MOORE RUBLE YUDELL CAMPUS & COMMUNITY BOOK PRODUCTION

Drawing Team: Tony Tran, Erica Moon, Richard Williams, Wing-Hon Ng, Richard Destin, Don Aitken, Angel Gabriel, James Jackson, Timothy Eng, Roger Lopez, Will Sheppird, Richard Ayers Jr.
Watercolor Renderings: Al Forster, Tony Tran
Special Thanks: Mark Denton, Stephen Harby, Asha Moorthy, Tony Tran

RODES HOUSE

Los Angeles, California
1977–1979

ST. MATTHEW'S EPISCOPAL CHURCH

Pacific Palisades, California
1979–1983

KWEE HOUSE

Singapore
1980–1985

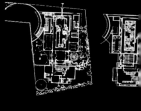

TEGEL HARBOR HOUSING

Berlin, Germany
Competition 1980
Phase I 1981–1988
Phase II 1981–present (in progress)

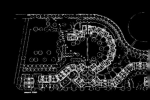

TEGEL HARBOR VILLA

Berlin, Germany
1985–1989

HUMBOLDT BIBLIOTHEK

Berlin, Germany
1984–1988

PARADOR HOTEL
San Juan Capistrano, California
1982 (Project)

MARINE STREET HOUSE
Santa Monica, California
1981–1983

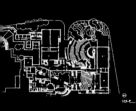

SAN ANTONIO ART INSTITUTE
San Antonio, Texas
1982–1989

**ST. LOUIS ART MUSEUM
WEST WING RENOVATION AND NEW
DECORATIVE ARTS GALLERIES**
St. Louis, Missouri
1983–1987

CAROUSEL PARK
Santa Monica Pier, Santa Monica, California
Competition 1984
1984–1987

INMAN HOUSE
Atlanta, Georgia
1984–1987

PLAZA LAS FUENTES
Pasadena, California
Phase I 1983–1989

BEL AIR PRESBYTERIAN CHURCH
Los Angeles, California
1984–1993

UNIVERSITY OF OREGON SCIENCE COMPLEX
Eugene, Oregon
1985–1989

ANAWALT HOUSE
Malibu, California
1985–1988

1992 CHICAGO WORLD'S FAIR
Chicago, Illinois
1986 (Project)

THE PETER BOXENBAUM ARTS EDUCATION CENTRE, CROSSROADS SCHOOL
Santa Monica, California
1986–1988

NATIVITY CATHOLIC CHURCH
Rancho Santa Fe, California
1985–1989

UCSD CELLULAR AND MOLECULAR MEDICINE WEST WING
University of California, San Diego, California
1986–1989

FIRST CHURCH OF CHRIST, SCIENTIST
Glendale, California
1986–1989

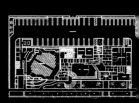

PLAYA VISTA MASTER PLAN
Los Angeles, California
1987–present (in progress)

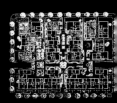

YODELL/BELBE HOUSE
Malibu, California
1987–1989

WALTER A. HAAS SCHOOL OF BUSINESS
University of California, Berkeley, California
1987–1995

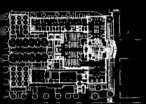

POWELL LIBRARY SEISMIC RENOVATION
University of California, Los Angeles, California
1988–1996

NISHIOKAMOTO HOUSING
Kobe, Japan
Phases I & II 1988–1992
Phase III 1994–1996

POTATISÄKERN HOUSING
Malmö, Sweden
1988–1996

CALIFORNIA CENTER FOR THE ARTS, ESCONDIDO
Escondido, California
1987–1994

UNIVERSITY OF WASHINGTON CHEMISTRY BUILDING

Tacoma, Washington
1988–1995

MALIBU HOUSING

Malibu, California
1988 (project)

BOLLE CENTER

Berlin, Germany
1990 (project)

VILLA SUPERBA

Venice, California
1990–1993

SCHETTER HOUSE

Pacific Palisades, California
1991–1994

UCSD CELLULAR AND MOLECULAR MEDICINE, EAST WING

University of California, San Diego, California
1991–1995

FRIEDRICHSTADT PASSAGEN

Berlin, Germany
1991 (project)

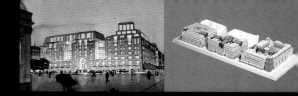

UNIVERSITY OF WASHINGTON TACOMA CAMPUS MASTER PLAN AND FIRST PHASE DESIGN

Tacoma, Washington
1991–present (in construction)

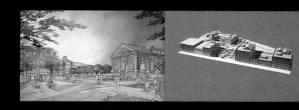

BERLINERSTRASSE HOUSING

Potsdam, Germany
1991–present (in construction)

KIRCHSTEIGFELD MASTER PLAN & HOUSING

Berlin, Germany
Competition 1992
1993–present (in construction)

PEEK & CLOPPENBURG DEPARTMENT STORE

Berlin, Germany
1992 (project)

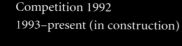

PEEK & CLOPPENBURG DEPARTMENT STORE

Leipzig, Germany
Competition 1992
1992–1994

DONG-HWA NATIONAL UNIVERSITY MASTER PLAN

Hwa-Lien, Taiwan
Competition 1992
1992–present (in construction)

AVERY HOUSE

California Institute of Technology, Pasadena, California
Competition 1992
1992–1996

KONSTANCIN HOUSING
Warsaw, Poland
1993–1996

THE HUGH AND HAZEL DARLING LAW LIBRARY ADDITION
University of California, Los Angeles, California
1992–present (in construction)

WALROD HOUSE
Berkeley, California
1992–1994

KAROW MASTER PLAN & HOUSING
Weissensee, Germany
Competition 1992
1992–present (in construction)

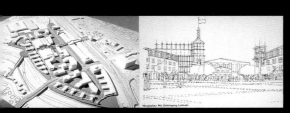

SHERMAN M. FAIRCHILD LIBRARY OF ENGINEERING AND APPLIED SCIENCE
California Institute of Technology, Pasadena, California
1993–present (in construction)

GÖTTINGEN MASTER PLAN
Göttingen, Germany
1993–present (in progress)

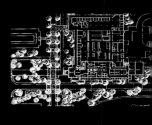

CENTER FOR INTEGRATED SYSTEMS EXPANSION
Stanford University, California
1993 (project)

MASTER PLAN AND STUDENT CENTER
Lewis & Clark College, Portland, Oregon
1993 (project)

KAO-SHIUNG INSTITUTE OF TECHNOLOGY CAMPUS MASTER PLAN DESIGN
Kao-Shiung, Taiwan
1993 (project)

MARYLAND CENTER FOR PERFORMING ARTS
University of Maryland, College Park, Maryland
Competition 1994
1994–present (in construction)

SHANGHAI GRAND THEATRE
Shanghai, People's Republic of China
1994 (project)

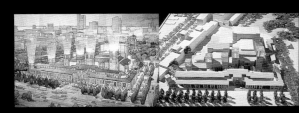

GRADUATE SCHOOL OF BUSINESS RESIDENTIAL LEARNING CENTER
Stanford University, California
1995 (project)

ULUDAG SKI RESORT
Bursa, Turkey
1995–present (in construction)

UNITED STATES EMBASSY
Berlin, Germany
Competition 1995
1995–present (in progress)

JOHN RUBLE

EDUCATION
University of California, Los Angeles, School of Architecture and Urban Planning,
Master of Architecture degree received 1976
University of Virginia, Bachelor of Architecture degree received 1969

TEACHING EXPERIENCE
Lecturer, University of California, Los Angeles, School of Architecture and Urban
Planning, 1981–present
Visiting Lecturer, Cornell University, 1976
Teaching Associate, University of California, Los Angeles, School of Architecture and
Urban Planning, 1975

PROFESSIONAL EXPERIENCE
Principal, Moore Ruble Yudell, Santa Monica, California, 1977–present
Associated with Charles W. Moore, Los Angeles, 1976–1977
Project Manager, Urban Innovations Group, Los Angeles, 1976–1977
Associated with O. M. Ungers, Ithaca, New York, 1976
Designer, Uniplan, Princeton, New Jersey, 1971–1975
Urban Designer, Peace Corps, Tunisia Kasserine Bureau d'Urbanisme, Ministre
de Tourisme et l'Amenagement du Territoire, 1969–1970

DISTINCTIONS/SERVICE
Lecture, Lawrence Technological University, Southfield, Michigan, 1993
"Dualities," Lecture with Buzz Yudell, College of Environmental Design, University
of California, Berkeley, 1993
Rancho Mirage Civic Center Competition Jury, 1992
Orange County AIA Design Awards Jury, 1991
Dean's Award for Distinguished Service, UCLA School of Architecture
and Urban Planning, 1976

BUZZ YUDELL

EDUCATION
Yale School of Architecture, Master of Architecture degree received 1973
Yale College, Bachelor of Arts cum laude degree received 1969

TEACHING EXPERIENCE
Adjunct Professor, University of California, Los Angeles, School of Architecture
and Urban Planning, 1977 to present
Visiting Critic, Technical University of Nova Scotia, Halifax School of Architecture, 1983
Visiting Critic, University of Texas at Austin School of Architecture, 1981
Visiting Critic in Architectural Design, Yale School of Architecture, 1972–1976

PROFESSIONAL EXPERIENCE
Principal, Moore Ruble Yudell, Santa Monica, California, 1977–present
Designer, Project Manager, Charles Moore Architect, Los Angeles California, 1976–1977
Project Manager, Urban Innovations Group, Los Angeles, California, 1976–1977
Principal, General Electric, New Haven, Connecticut, 1974–1976
Evans Wollen Architects, Hotchkiss, Connecticut (site office), 1973
Charles W. Moore Associates/Moore Grover Harper, Essex Connecticut, 1972–1973

SELECTED PUBLISHED WRITING
"Collisions of the Ideal and the Uncertain," *Space Design* No. 266, November, 1986
"Moore in Progress," *Global Architecture* No. 7, Tokyo 1980
Body, Memory and Architecture, contributor with Charles W. Moore and Kent
Bloomer, 1977
"Architecture 1976," with Charles W. Moore, *Funk & Wagnalls 1976 Encyclopedia
Yearbook*, New York
"Architecture 1973," with Charles W. Moore, *Funk & Wagnalls 1973 Encyclopedia
Yearbook*, New York

MOORE RUBLE YUDELL: SELECTED AWARDS AND DISTINCTIONS

United States Institute for Theater Technology, Merit Award, 1995, California Center for the Arts, Escondido
Concrete Masonry Design Award, Molecular Biology Research Facility, Unit II, 1994
American Institute of Architects, Interiors Award, Nativity Catholic Church, 1993
Interior Award, *Interiors Magazine*, Nativity Catholic Church, 1992
California Council, American Institute of Architects, Firm of the Year Award, 1992
California Council, American Institute of Architects, Urban Design Award, 1992, Plaza Las Fuentes, Pasadena, California
California Council, American Institute of Architects, Honor Award, 1992, Yudell/Beebe House, Malibu
American Library Association/AIA Library Building Award, 1991, Humboldt Library
San Diego Chapter, American Institute of Architects, Honor Award, 1991, Nativity Catholic Church
American Wood Council, Honor Award, 1991
First Church of Christ, Scientist, Glendale, California
California Council, American Institute of Architects, Honor Award, 1991, First Church of Christ, Scientist, Glendale
American Institute of Architects/American Library Council Award, 1990, Humboldt Library
Los Angeles Chapter, American Insitute of Architects, Honor Award, 1990, Humboldt Library
California Council, American Institute of Architects, Merit Award, 1989, House on Point Dume
American Institute of Architects Honor Award, 1988 Tegel Harbor Housing
California Council, American Institute of Architects, Honor Award, 1988, Tegel Harbor Housing
California Council, American Institute of Architects, Honor Award, 1988, Carousel Park
Building a Better Future Honor Award, 1987 (State of California Department of Rehabilitation Architectural Design Awards Program) Carousel Park
City of Santa Monica Mayor's Commendation, October, 1987, Carousel Park
Excellence on the Waterfront Honor Award, Waterfront Center, 1987, Carousel Park
American Institute of Architects Honor Award, 1984, St. Matthew's Church
California Council, American Institute of Architects, Merit Award, 1984, St. Matthew's Church
Los Angeles Chapter, American Institute of Architects, Merit Award, 1984, St. Matthew's Church
Architectural Record House of the Year, 1981, Rodes House
First Prize, Santa Monica Pier Design Charrette, 1981
First Prize, Tegel Harbor International Design Competition, West Berlin 1980
Exhibition, Max Protetch Gallery, NYC 1980, St. Matthew's Church
"Contemporary Views of the House," Mandeville Gallery, University of California San Diego 1983
"The California Condition," La Jolla Museum of Contemporary Art, 1982

MOORE RUBLE YUDELL: SELECTED EXHIBITIONS

"Transitions: Work in Progress by Moore Ruble Yudell," UCLA School of Architecture and Urban Planning, 1995
"Der Revision der Moderne Postmodern, Architecture 1960–1980," Deutschen Architecturmuseum, Frankfurt, West Germany, 1984
"Das Abenteuer der Ideen," National Galerie, Berlin, West Germany, 1984
"Contemporary Views of the House," Mandeville Gallery, University of California San Diego, 1983
"The California Condition," La Jolla Museum of Contemporary Art, 1982

SELECTED PUBLISHED WORK

"A Last Act: Taking Whimsy to School," *The New York Times*, November 26, 1995 Haas School of Business
"The AD 100," *Architectural Digest*, September 1995
"Hail to the Haas," *San Jose Mercury News*, May 7, 1995, Haas School of Business
The New American House, Whitney Library of Design, 1995 Yudell/Beebe House
California Gardens, Clarkson N. Potter, Inc., 1995, Yudell/Beebe House
"Arts Fusion," *Architecture*, December 1994, California Center for the Arts, Escondido
Moore Ruble Yudell: Houses and Housing, AIA Press, 1994
Architects House Themselves: Breaking New Ground, The Preservation Press, 1994, Yudell/Beebe House
"Building for the Arts", *Arch*, December, 1994
Museum Builders, Academy Editions, 1994, various projects
School Design, Van Nostrand Reinhold, 1994, University of Oregon Science Complex

World Cities: Los Angeles, Academy Editions, 1994, various projects
"Moore Ruble Yudell: A Firm on the Go," *The World & I*, July 1994
Moore Ruble Yudell, Academy Editions, 1993
"Moore Ruble Yudell, 1979–1982," *Architecture and Urbanism*, August 1992
"Earthly Delights, A California design couple's country idyll" (cover), *House Beautiful*, August 1992
"Outdoor Rooms" (cover), *Elle Decor*, April/May 1992
"University of Oregon Science Complex," *Arch*, March/April 1992
"Nishiokamoto Housing," *Arch*, January/February, 1992
"Designers of the Year," *Interiors*, January 1992, Nativity Catholic Church
"Science Fair" (cover), *Architectural Record*, November 1991 University of Oregon Science Complex
"1991–1992 Western Home Awards, Award of Merit" (cover), *Sunset Magazine*, October 1991
"Feature Story: The Custom Collection" (cover), *Builder*, June 1991
"Tegel Harbor Housing," *Arch*, May/June 1991
"Humboldt Bibliotek" (cover), *American Libraries*, April 1991
"Collaborative Genius," "Angeleno Gothic," "Campus Medicine," *Architecture*, March 1991
"John Ruble, MRY," *Berlin Architecture Year Book*, 1991
"Malibu on their Minds" (cover), *House and Garden*, February 1991
"A Place Apart" (cover), *Architectural Record*, February 1991, Nativity Catholic Church
"Bel Air Presbyterian Church" (cover), *American Organist*, February, 1991
"University of Oregon Science Complex" (cover), *Places*, Volume 7, Number 4, 1991
"Moore Ruble Yudell: A Malibu Residence," *Architectural Digest*, February 1990, House on Point Dume
"Pride of Place," *Architectural Record*, January 1990, Humboldt Library
The Backyard Book, Viking Penguin, Inc., 1988, King Studio
"Waterfront Housing at Once Exuberant and Classical," *Architecture*, May 1988, Tegel Harbor Housing
"Berlino 1988," *Abitare*, May 1988, Milano, Italy, Tegel Harbor
"Housing That's Changing the Face of West Berlin," *The New York Times*, April 14, 1988, Tegel Harbor
"Living by the Water" (cover), *Progressive Architecture*, October 1987, Tegel Harbor Housing
"Moore Ruble Yudell: Remodeling a Spanish Colonial House in Beverly Hills" (cover), *Architectural Digest*, September 1987, Pynoos House
"Charles Moore" (cover), *Interiors*, September 1987, St. Matthew's Church, Church of the Nativity, Humboldt Library
"Rebuilding Berlin, Yet Again," *Time*, June 15, 1987, Tegel Harbor Housing
"Das Pathos endet an der Haustür," *Der Spiegel*, June 1, 1987, Tegel Harbor Housing
American Houses, Philip Langdon, New York: Stewart, Tabori & Chang, 1987, King Studio, Marine Street Residence
"Perfection in Miniature," *House Beautiful*, February 1987, King Studio
Freestyle, Tim Street-Porter, New York: Stewart, Tabori & Chang, 1986, Rodes House, Marine Street Residence
Charles Moore, Buildings and Projects 1949–1986, Eugene J. Johnson, ed., New York: Rizzoli, 1986, St. Matthew's Church, Tegel Harbor Housing, Humboldt Library, San Juan Capistrano Library
"Overview of Recent Works," *Space Design*, November 1986, Tegel Harbor, Plaza Las Fuentes, The Parador Hotel, St. Matthew's Church, San Antonio Art Institute, Kwee House
"Architecture: Moore Ruble Yudell," *Architectural Digest*, August 1985, Kwee House
"Built on Religious, Regional Tradition, St. Matthew's Church," *Architecture*, May 1984, Washington, D.C.
"Design by Congregation," *Architectural Record*, February 1984, St. Matthew's Church
"St. Matthew's Parish Church," *Architecture + Urbanism*, January 1984
Erste Projekte, Internationale Bauausstellung Berlin 1984, West Berlin 1981, Tegel Harbor
"A Church Is Not a Home," *Newsweek*, March 1983, St. Matthew's Church
"Charles Moore: Recent Projects," *Architectural Review*, August 1981, London
"Back to the Classics," *Newsweek*, September 1981, New York, Rodes House
"Houses of the Year," *Architectural Record*, May 1981, Rodes House
"New American Architecture 1981," *Architecture + Urbanism*, 1981, Tokyo
"Palladio Lives On," *Life*, December 1980, New York, Rodes House
"Charles Moore and Company," *Global Architecture* No. 7, Tokyo 1981

COLOR AND GARDEN DESIGNER

TINA BEEBE

While still in college, Tina Beebe worked with Charles Moore and later joined his firm in Essex, Connecticut. She received her M.F. A. from the Yale School of Art and Architecture and formed a design firm with Buzz Yudell in New Haven, Connecticut. She and Buzz came to California to work with Charles Moore in 1976. She worked as well in the office of Charles and Ray Eames, learning much from her great friend and mentor, Ray Eames.

Tina combines influences from all of these experiences with her own fascination with color as resident colorist for Moore Ruble Yudell. She has designed the color for almost every project Moore Ruble Yudell has built. She also consults extensively for distinguished U.S. and international architecture firms.

Recently Tina has combined her love of gardening with her design and color abilities to create gardens, both residential and commercial. She finds plants inspire her color palette and colors evoke ideas for whole gardens, and these in turn reflect and extend the colors of Moore Ruble Yudell's buildings.

ASSOCIATES

MARK DENTON

Mark Denton began his association with Charles Moore in 1979, taking time from his studies in architecture at Yale to work on community planning and development in Springfield, Massachusetts, and Watkins Glen, New York. In both these projects, techniques were employed to encourage community involvement and participation in the planning process, including a series of local call-in prime time live television shows. This experience led to responsibility for programming a new city hall and civic offices for the city of Sacramento.

Since joining Moore Ruble Yudell, Mark has directed the firm's business development and has been involved in a variety of institutional projects. On the design team for the Walter A. Haas School of Business at the University of California, Berkeley, Mark led participatory design workshops, later concentrating on the business school program and conceptual design. He led the programming effort for the chemistry building at the University of Washington, Seattle and is Associate-in-Charge for the Avery House student/faculty residence at California Institute of Technology. Mark became an associate of Moore Ruble Yudell in 1990.

MICHAEL DE VILLIERS

Michael de Villiers was born in South Africa and received his undergraduate education in architecture at the University of Cape Town. After graduating, he worked on several commercial and house projects in Cape Town. He obtained his M.Arch. at UCLA and joined Moore Ruble Yudell in 1987.

As project architect for the UCLA Powell Library renovation and Law School Library addition, he has worked on issues of seismic and historical renovation, and at the University of Washington new branch campus in Tacoma, on issues of adaptive reuse. He has managed all phases of project development, and has led several projects through construction. He has a particular interest in housing issues, and is currently working on design of the Sea Castle/Ocean Hotel apartments in Santa Monica, and on studies for new residential neighborhoods at Mission Bay, San Francisco. Another current responsibility is design of a new phase of an office campus at Solana, near Dallas, Texas. His experience also includes the Church of the Nativity and the Cellular and Molecular Medicine research laboratory at the University of California, San Diego.

DANIEL GARNESS

Daniel Garness has been a project manager at Moore Ruble Yudell for ten years and is an associate with the firm. His most recent assignments have been as Project Manager and Designer for several large projects in Berlin, including master planning for 5,000 units of new housing and infrastructure on the edge of the city and a luxury housing project in Potsdam, Germany. Previously he was project landscape designer on a 20-acre condominium project in Kobe, Japan, and project manager and designer on a large multi-family residential project in Malibu, California. He was project manager and designer for Plaza Las Fuentes, a 500,000-square-foot mixed-use development in Pasadena, including a 365-room hotel and extensive public gardens, completed in 1988. Dan's experience includes large-scale site planning and environmental design, housing design, and residential design.

ASSOCIATES'
BIOGRAPHIES

STEPHEN HARBY

Stephen Harby worked in association with Charles Moore before joining Moore Ruble Yudell in 1984. This experience included managing the design teams for several major civic and institutional projects, as well as collaboration on a number of smaller projects. Stephen has acted as Project Manager for the University of Oregon Science Complex, completed in 1989, the renovation and expansion of a Beverly Hills residence, the Walter A. Haas School of Business Administration, completed in 1995, and the University of Washington Chemistry Building, also completed in 1995. He has been the Associate-in-Charge of the University of Washington Tacoma Campus Master Plan, now under construction, and also served in that role for the UCLA Law School Library additions and the Sherman Fairchild Applied Science and Engineering Library at the California Institute of Technology. He has lectured and consulted in India on campus planning and historic preservation.

A graduate of Yale University and Yale School of Architecture, Stephen's interests include architectural history and travel. He was among the firm's first associates, named in 1991, and has served on a number of boards and commissions, including the Santa Monica Landmarks Commission and the Board of Directors of the Southern California Chapter of the Society of Architectural Historians.

VIRGINIA C. MARSHALL

Virginia Marshall has been office manager at Moore Ruble Yudell since 1983. Having overseen the growth of the front office from a one-person position into a full clerical staff, Virginia now focuses on staff management and finance. She has been an associate since 1990. Virginia attended North Park College in Chicago. Outside the office, Virginia is an active community volunteer and has bicycled the West Coast from Canada to Mexico and the United States from shore to shore.

NEAL S. MATSUNO

Neal Matsuno has been with Moore Ruble Yudell for over ten years, having joined the firm shortly after graduating from the University of Southern California in 1984. He was named an associate in 1996. As a project manager, Neal combines design sensitivity with skills in technical coordination throughout the design process. His areas of special expertise include lighting design and specifications, and he played a major role in the lighting design for the California Center for the Arts in Escondido, which was the recipient of the GE Edison Award of Excellence.

Neal has had a major responsibility for technical detailing, consultant coordination, lighting design, and specifications for the California Center for the Arts in Escondido, Powell Library, and Law Library projects at UCLA. Neal is the Associate-in-Charge of the 1,087-acre mixed-use Playa Vista Project consisting of office space, housing, schools, recreation areas, and restored wetlands.

JAMES B. MORTON

James B. Morton was an engineer for ten years before embarking on his career as an architect. Upon obtaining his M. Arch. degree from UCLA, he joined Charles Moore's team for the Beverly Hills Civic Center, where he was the project manager for the performing arts theater, library renovation, and parking structure. In 1984, he came to Moore Ruble Yudell, where he co-managed the design of the University of Oregon Science Complex. Other project management assignments included the feasibility study for the seismic renovation of Powell Library, master planning for the Rand Corporation site in Santa Monica, design of the Ocean Avenue Hotel and Office Buildings, design for Kobe Nishiokamoto Housing in Kobe, Japan, and the California Center for the Arts, Escondido. As Project Director for the California Center for the Arts, Jim led the project staff, including four project teams for individual buildings, through all phases of design and production. Jim is currently the Associate-in-Charge of the Maryland Center for Performing Arts, with five performance halls, a performing arts library, and academic space for the music, drama, and dance departments. Jim has been an associate since 1990.

JAMES MARY O'CONNOR

Born and raised in Dublin, Ireland, James Mary O'Connor came to participate in Charles Moore's Master Studios at UCLA in 1982 as a Fulbright Scholar. James also studied with Buzz Yudell while at UCLA. He has been with Moore Ruble Yudell for the past ten years and is an Associate.

James has served as Project Architect and Designer for several large projects, notably the Kobe Nishiokamoto Housing in Japan, the Maryland Center for Performing Arts, Konstancin Housing in Poland, and Peek & Cloppenburg Department Store in Berlin, and he has worked extensively on competition projects. Recently, James has edited and been very involved in publications of the office's work, including *Moore Ruble Yudell* (Academy Editions, 1992), *Houses and Housing* (Rockport/AIA, 1993), and *Campus and Community* (Rockport/AIA, 1996).

James received his B.Sc. Architecture cum laude from Trinity College in Dublin, his Dip. Arch. from the Dublin Institute for Technology, and his Master of Architecture from UCLA. He currently teaches a design studio at UCLA's Interior and Environmental Design Program and has served as guest critic and lecturer at USC School of Architecture, Woodbury University Department of Architecture, and the Dublin Institute of Technology.

CECILY YOUNG

Born in Los Angeles, Cecily Young studied at the College of Environmental Design at Berkeley, receiving her Master of Architecture in 1983. She has traveled and studied abroad extensively, including a year of architecture study at the Polytechnic of Central London in 1976 and the International Laboratory for Architecture and Urban Design in Siena in 1982. Before joining Moore Ruble Yudell in 1986, her work covered the spectrum from building inspector in Oakland to urban designer with the Redevelopment Agency of San Jose. Her work at Moore Ruble Yudell began with the planning of the conference hotel at Plaza Las Fuentes, Pasadena. As Project Architect, Cecily has directed projects of significant size, including Friedrichstadt Passagen, a competition project for mixed-use development in the heart of Berlin; All Saints North Quadrangle, a day care and church administrative center; Peek & Cloppenburg Leipzig, a competition winning department store completed recently in the historic center of Leipzig, Germany; Potatisåkern master plan and design for housing in Malmö, Sweden; and a competition for the U.S. Embassy in Berlin.

It has been a delight to collaborate with a broad spectrum of talented colleagues on the publication of this book. Indeed, the contributions of many individuals in a highly collaborative process reflect an important theme: the creation of community through collegial dialogue.

Oscar Riera Ojeda has gone beyond normal expectations of work as a designer, with great passion for the issues and the objects of architecture. His perseverance and commitment have been matched by his thoughtfulness and sensitivity to the subject at hand. Rockport Publishers, under the direction of Stanley Patey, assisted by Acquisitions Editor Rosalie Grattaroti, Editorial/Marketing Director Winnie Danenbarger, and Senior Editor Don Fluckinger, has continued in its commitment to architecture and urbanism as important areas for public consideration and discussion. They have brought to bear the highest standards of editorial excellence, with equal concern for content and form. John Ray Hoke and the AIA Press have generously supported this effort. Without the commitment and dedication of our editors, James Mary O'Connor and Wendy Kohn, this book would not have been a reality. Our Associate, James Mary O'Connor, exuberantly and skillfully guided the process from the conception through the final details of publication. Wendy Kohn brought her keen intellect and literary experience to conceptualizing the book's format, and editing our writing as well as that of the contributors. Special thanks to Timothy Hursley, for his extraordinary photographs.

We feel a special gratitude for the splendid efforts of our many colleagues, all of whom are enormously busy professionals in architecture or architectural criticism. Witold Rybczynski has thoughtfully established the context for this book by his insights into the societal meanings and humanistic principles of college as a "world apart," an "interlude between adolescence and adult life." Stefanos Polyzoides has written an exceptional essay that lays both historic and typologic foundations for the understanding of "campus making in America." (His essay represents more than the seed of a volume unto itself.)

Diane Favro has brought the insight of an historian and the passion of a Berkeley alumna to her analysis of the Haas School of Business. Donlyn Lyndon has combined the insights of a life-long educator, architect, and urbanist to his reflections on the University of Oregon. Rob Quigley demonstrates the thoughtfulness of a practicing architect with an expanding concern for campus and urban issues. Our Associate Stephen Harby contributed eloquently both as project architect and writer in his description of work at the University of Washington. We feel fortunate to have had as both clients and friends Duke Oakley, who has led the renaissance in campus planning at UCLA, and Roger Lewis and Steven Hurtt, who are leading a similar charge at the University of Maryland. We have especially enjoyed a long association with Tallman Trask, who has directed a new collection of projects at the University of Washington's Seattle campus while laying the foundations for the new campus at Tacoma. This remarkable group of colleagues has brought the combined sensitivities of educators, administrators, and architects; a special understanding that grows from aspirations annealed by years in the trenches.

Our work would not have the depth and richness that we hope we are achieving without the extraordinary efforts of our associates and staff. Similarly, an intense collaboration with our many consultants and clients has contributed to the truly communal effort upon which all of our efforts rest. We thank all of you for your individual and collective creativity and for the opportunity to build community together.

Buzz Yudell   John Ruble

NOTE FROM THE ARCHITECTS